GW01035667

Knockmore garden in spring was something out of this world. We had never seen masses of bulbs coming up through the grass under fruit trees just bursting with blossom. We had never seen terraces with pergolas and Italian vases full of flowers . . . we had never seen such a garden built in the cup of the hills, with a peep through the woods of the distant sea. . . .

Phoebe Whitworth, niece of the Miss Mays, original designers of the garden, remembering her visit in 1906

A Year in an Irish Garden

Ruth Isabel Ross

Illustrated by
Jeremy Williams

A. & A. Farmar

British Library cataloguing in Publication Data
A CIP catalogue record for this book is available from the
British Library

Illustrations by Jeremy Williams
Cover design by Jarlath Hayes
Text designed and set by A. & A. Farmar
Printed and bound by ColourBooks

ISBN (HB) 1-899047-63-8

First published in 1999
by
A. & A. Farmar
Beech House
78 Ranelagh Village
Dublin 6
Ireland
Tel: +353 1 496 3625
Fax: + 353 1 497 0107
Email: afarmar@iol.ie
Web: farmarbooks.com

Contents

Acknowledgements

I am grateful to Mrs Margaret Osmaston and to Timothy Whitworth for allowing me to quote extracts from their mother Phoebe Whitworth's memoirs 'View from the Peak'.

I would also like to thank Sandy Dunbar and Catherine Porteous as well as all the other friends and relations of the Miss Mays who have recounted happy episodes at Knockmore.

Especial thanks to my husband, John. In spite of being an inveterate traveller he has stayed at home to help reconstruct the garden and has made it all possible.

Ruth Isabel Ross
Knockmore
September 1999

Introduction

The place

Knockmore is a pretty, regency-style house in north County Wicklow. In front, facing east, its two green fields slope down towards the sea, three miles away. A hundred yards from the house on the south side is a wood full of oak, beech and cherry trees with an under-growth of hazel. Between the wood and the house is a hollow where, many years ago, a garden was made.

The history

Not much is known of Knockmore's history until 1898 when Charlotte May and her sister Stella, the Miss Mays

Knockmore

1

as they were called locally, came to live here. A few features can be identified from before their time, a dog's grave dated 1887, a generous planting of Spanish chestnut trees, *Castanea sativa,* now magnificent, on one perimeter of the lower field.

We do know that the Miss Mays, with the help of two men and a boy, transformed Knockmore's small valley into a garden with all the features of a horticultural golden age. There were beds of old roses, a double herbaceous border, dry wall terraces, lily ponds, a pergola walk and a glade for wild flowers. There were prolific crops of vegetables and fruit. Charlotte May's feelings for the place were so intense that she threatened to haunt any future owner who did not look after the garden. So far we have never seen her . . . The Miss Mays lived at Knockmore for fifty years.

The garden

We have kept the old divisions: it would have been insensitive, if not impossible, to uproot the fine beech and holly hedges or to break up paths built with such a sound hardcore.

We have continued planting with zest. Our perennials, shrubs and old roses are mainly well known favourites, chosen carefully for harmony of colour. The great designer, Gertrude Jekyll, thought this harmony was the key to a restful garden, so that at Knockmore, after mid-June, orange, scarlet and strong yellow flowers are forbidden, while crimson and deep blue ones

The wood, looking west

tone in with their paler shades. All are lightened by occasional groups of silver leaved plants. As the soil is not acid no camellias, rhododendrons or azaleas are planted.

The garden now consists of—

The wild garden Formed from an irregular triangle in the lowest part of the hollow. It is full of wild flowers, woodland ones like anemones, bluebells, primroses, foxgloves and Welsh poppies. There are informal ponds, unusual trees and a dogs' graveyard.

The summer garden A rectangle, with a formal lily pond, an old sundial, and a double border full of herbaceous plants, shrubs and old roses. Deep steps rise up into the darkness of the wood.

The kitchen garden A formal and productive vegetable garden, also some soft fruit in rows.

The rosebeds Two small box-edged beds of shrub roses, most of them French, underplanted with catmint. Rose colours are mainly pale pink or white but are enriched by shades of crimson.

The gravel garden In a sunny corner near the house. Plants, green, blue and grey-leaved, roll onto gravel and some are planted into the stones: more have seeded themselves there and are encouraged if we like them.

The high walk, formerly a pergola walk The pergola collapsed thirty-five years ago. We have planted the edge of the walk with a long lavender bed: from this path there is now a panoramic view of the garden.

The dark walk Old gardens often had dark or shady walks for people to enjoy on bright days without damaging their complexions. This one is bordered with ferns and leads towards a stone bench. For some forgotten reason the walk is called simply 'The Elizabethan' though there is nothing remotely Elizabethan about it.

The wood Has been acquired since the Miss Mays lived
here. Paths from the garden wind round deciduous
trees and up and down dells. There are rocky out-
crops and dramatic glimpses of the Dargle Valley.
Squirrels, rabbits and hedgehogs live in the wood.

The People

John and I are the owners of Knockmore.

We are fortunate in the friends and helpers who frequently appear in our story—

Mervyn chief gardener and source of help in so many
other ways.

Sheila who keeps the borders in good shape in summer

Jimmy the ever reliable cutter of grass and skilful
amputator of tree branches.

Rosemary a neighbour, friend and mentor.

Maureen who keeps the house alive when the garden
takes over.

Unfortunate relatives and friends who come to stay in
summer and find themselves roped in to dead-head
roses or pick fruit and vegetables.

Groups of visitors, who by coming from all over to admire the garden provide us with a constant stimulus.

And,

Not exactly people but friends anyway Cora, a young Cairn
terrier, the bane of rabbits and Alexander, a very old
tortoiseshell cat, scourge of rats.

January

1 January

There will be no New Year resolutions made for this garden today. Not a single one. Last year we made dozens. Paths would be sprayed with weedkiller every first Monday of the month, narrow borders hoed every week and apples thinned in June, without fail. There were many more, too many. It inevitably poured with rain each weedkilling Monday, the weeks flew by without a chance of hoeing, and June was too strenuous for us even to look at the apple crop. This year we shall be flexible, so will not feel guilty about broken resolutions.

We have never tried to make a winter garden. In spite of this, I find life in the little borders in front of the house this New Year's Day. There are groups of pretty *Cyclamen coum* in flower, a spread of lungwort in bud and a Christmas rose nearly in bloom. The mophead hydrangeas have not yet lost last year's now greenish flowers.

It is too grey a day for the Algerian irises, they bloom

only in the sun, but down the garden path, white-flowered periwinkle romps over a bank. The summer garden is now a frost pocket and icy cold, but near the wood a clump of snowdrops is almost open, and hard-by a Corsican hellebore flowers.

On the high walk our nine winter jasmine plants are in full flower. They were layered from a single bush a few years ago, and now their soft yellow colour cheers us through the dark winter months when we have to light up by four o'clock.

6 January

A freezing day drives us in to sit by the winter room fire where our logs, well organised by John, are burning brightly. For thirty years all our firewood has been cut from fallen trees or branches, then seasoned for twelve months. We are working through our Thompson and Morgan seed catalogue and dreaming of summer.

We are concentrating on seeds for the kitchen garden. We must because we described it as 'unusual' in our account of the place for visitors who should not be disappointed. Last year John designed the eight rectangular beds centred round a small granite table. We know no other plot like it, tidyish but not rigid, with pyramids of sweet peas emerging from the smaller crops. Luckily the useful but hideous cabbage family find our soil too thin: more exotic plants thrive.

We always grow broad beans and scarlet runners. This year we will embark on both golden and black

dwarf beans and will hope desperately for a warm May to cherish them. (The black ones turn luscious green in boiling water.) We are sowing seeds of plum tomatoes, red and yellow, for roasting as well as small cherry ones for sweetness. We will grow yellow courgettes, strangely shaped, as well as long green ones. Florence fennel will be sown after midsummer to prevent it from going to seed in the long days. We will choose redskinned onions and reddish lettuce: the colour red is supposed to give extra nourishment and certainly enlivens rows of vegetables.

We will follow the fashion of including cut flowers in the kitchen garden. Two rows of cosmos, one white-flowered and one crimson, will supplement the pyramids of sweet peas giving us simple flower arrangements

The kitchen garden from the high walk

9

for the summer and autumn.

Our order will be posted tomorrow.

10 January

The Algerian irises have come into their own today; they are blooming for the sun, several flowers on each plant. Since the flowers last only a day, I pick all that I can find to bring indoors; this will help future flowering. Our white-flowered irises are more rare, but we like the mauve ones better.

12 January

We walk through the dark walk to the wood. Winter is the season when we pay most attention to the trees, the ones in the wood and others round the perimeter of the garden. Most of the work is done carefully by Jimmy with his chainsaw. He is spending today cutting out dead wood. Every bit is sliced and laid on the ground to be removed to the back yard; there it will be cut into eighteen-inch logs to dry for next winter's fires. Jimmy is coppicing hazel from the wood too, to be made into garden fences. Our wood is an integral part of the garden, and an enticement to the red squirrels. We have never seen grey squirrels here.

15 January

This morning David, a tree surgeon, comes to examine the larger and older trees. They are in good order, he thinks. An ash tree has to come down because it shades the greenhouse. Other trees need to be fertilised and to have some branches removed.

17 January

David's estimate arrives. What a shock! We had forgotten the price of tree surgery and the imposition of VAT; now we wonder how anyone can afford it. We decide to have only the minimum done and on dangerous trees.

In the same post is a garden society letter from Kells, County Meath: a group of thirty would like to see the garden in June, our second booking for that month; the first was from a Swiss rose society. We love having groups in midsummer when most of the old roses are in flower. Our revered Miss Mays would be horrified at us for opening the garden commercially, even in the modest way we do. We do not feel guilty. The garden gives pleasure to so many and even helps the high grade tourism Ireland aims for. And there is no doubt that the occasional 'group visit' stimulates us to work hard: nothing could be better for the garden. This would please the Miss Mays.

23 January

Both John and Mervyn are fond of creating views. They make views of the sea, views of the Sugar Loaf mountain and even views down a shrubby bank to the wild garden daffodils. This can mean cutting down in half a minute a thirty-year-old tree or bush. Today they are discussing creating a distant glimpse of the sea from one of the paths at the top of the garden, a view treasured fifty years ago by the Miss Mays, and now obscured by cherry, oak and eucalyptus. Sometimes John is rash; at other times inspired. We come to the conclusion today that every view should have a frame and that trees and shrubs must be saved if at all possible.

It is diverting to notice the difference between men and women gardeners. Men like bold schemes, large plantations, striking follies, while women love individual plants and their nurture, with colours blended to give a sense of well-being. This is delightfully borne out by two books published by Chatto and Windus in the 1980s: *The Englishwoman's Garden* is a series of outdoor rooms, intimate, full of well-tended flowers. *The*

The view of the Sugar Loaf mountain from the gravel garden

Englishman's Garden is all bold extravagance, waterfalls, trees by the hundred and strange monuments.

Without men's vision there would be no long vistas in the Le Nôtre style at nearby Killruddery, none of Daniel Robertson's dramatic terracing at Powerscourt and no thrilling glimpses of the Mediterranean from La Mortola, the Hanbury garden, on the French–Italian border. The most popular women gardeners have been plantswomen—Jane Loudon, Vita Sackville West and Gertrude Jekyll—who all relied on men, in two cases their husbands, the third Edwin Lutyens, to provide the framework they filled with such well-chosen flowers. But at least two exceptional women have joined the ranks of famous landscape architects, Beatrice Farrand, creator of Dumbarton Oaks in Washington, DC, and Dame Sylvia Crowe, so bold with tree contours and author of *Forestry of the Landscape*.

26 January

Our garden birds feed mainly at one o'clock when we do. We are looking at them today from the kitchen window. Robins and sparrows are pecking at seeds on the home-made bird-table and blue tits are fluttering around the swinging half coconut. They all perch on the bare branches of a weeping cherry before feeding, making a lively scene. After some minutes of happy pecking, the little birds scatter in terror as a large hooded crow hops down from the great Spanish chestnut tree. Even the stolid magpies move off in their deliberate way.

30 January

We decide to humanise the wild garden. It sparkles with life in spring when the grass is studded with early flowers. After June, though, the scythed grass, the darkish leaves, the still water give a lifeless atmosphere. We can make the water trickle by the turn of a stopcock, but this is wasteful and done only for visitors. A sign of human activity is badly needed.

Even sitting down is human activity, but there is nowhere in the wild garden to place a seat: seats need walls or hedges close behind them and views in front. We wondered whether to put two elegant lead cranes by one of the ponds but they would look pretentious and would undoubtedly be stolen. So in the early spring John and Mervyn will make a simple bridge over one of the pond channels; they will need just two sturdy planks and a few lengths of coppiced hazel. It will be a pretty little feature and an invitation to cross over the ponds and take a mown path into the wood.

31 January

January has been cold and dark, and so perfectly normal. As usual, we have spent most of it indoors thinking and planning for the garden in summer. We go outside to exercise Cora, little older than a puppy, to explore the wood and to admire the jasmine walk; the tangle of yellow flowers tumbling down beside the terrace steps is especially brilliant this year. On sunny days we pick the winter irises. We long for the spring, but it seems far away.

Recipe for January:
Creamy Leek Soup

Leeks are still in our garden. This quickly made soup, from Scotland, is creamy but light, excellent as the first of three courses. The oatmeal and the leek make it a nourishing dish for the winter.

INGREDIENTS
Serves four

30 g/1 oz/1 tablespoon margarine or olive oil

1 medium-sized leek, finely chopped

2 tablespoons fine oatflakes

500 ml/1 pint chicken stock

1 tablespoon marjoram

1 tablespoon thyme

salt

freshly ground black pepper

250 ml/½ pint milk

1 tablespoon parsley, roughly chopped

4 tablespoons cream, optional

METHOD
Melt the margarine or oil over a very low heat.

Add the leek and oatflakes and cook gently for a few minutes without browning.

Add the chicken stock, herbs and a very little salt

and pepper. Bring this to the boil and simmer gently until the leek and oatmeal are cooked—about 20 minutes.

Liquidise this and warm it up again with the milk until it is hot but not boiling. Taste for seasoning and add the roughly chopped parsley. Serve at once.

Cream is not necessary; oatmeal makes the soup creamy. For those who like cream in soup, pour a tablespoonful of cream into each hot soup plate. Then add the soup and stir lightly to make a marbled effect.

February

The dell

1 February

It is a beautiful day, cold but still with a blue sky. The Kish lighthouse shines white, ten miles out in what looks like a Mediterranean sea. There is movement, just a little movement, in the garden. *Cyclamen coum*, lungwort and Christmas rose are blooming with self-confidence now in the cold front borders; they will soon be joined by dusty pink hellebores. There is a drift of a thousand or so blueish species crocuses under the Spanish chestnut tree opposite the kitchen window; they are just starting to flower.

The snowdrops are at their peak. The special ones on the south side of the summer garden grow in bare earth, and are nearly a foot high. The wild garden snowdrops, growing in grass, are shorter but look effective, rippling out from the foot of our giant cherry tree.

Shrubs and trees have moved a little. The winter sweet, *Chimonanthus fragrans*, is in bloom, and there are a few sweet-smelling blossoms on that most rewarding evergreen shrub, *Viburnum* X *burkwoodii*.

In the kitchen garden, rhubarb, invisible the last time we investigated, now shows an inch of crimson shoots under the old laminated tea chests which we use to force early growth.

3 February

Since there is brilliant sunshine, I go to have a close look at the drift of crocuses. All their thin petals are wide open as if to drink the sunlight; they will close tonight, but for the next two or three weeks will form a pale blue lake every sunny day.

These crocuses are blooming and spreading, doing everything they should, but are in an obscure place under our great Spanish chestnut tree. We would like to see some more.

Crocuses are a problem, mice eat the bulbs, birds

nip off the flowers and they are choosy about habitat. For the last few years we have been trying to make a large drift of *Crocus tommasinianus* in the wild garden but have had nothing but frustration and expense. Planting a hundred crocus bulbs every year in grass was like purgatory Mervyn said and he never complains. In they went but did the flowers come up? Only two or three of them.

Rosemary came to the rescue today by showing me a book of alpine wild flowers; the crocuses were growing out of grass, so sparse that it was hardly grass at all. The thick rank grass of our wild garden where other wild flowers abound is obviously death to crocuses.

I seemed to hear the brisk tones of Charlotte May tell me that it was absurd to grow crocuses in the wild garden. If it had been possible she would have done it. Snowdrops, anemones, daffodils, primroses, bluebells, Yes, but crocuses No, and fritillaries No. This was chastening but helpful.

We track down a fragrant scent on the wild garden side of the holly hedge, the obscure but sweet-smelling sarcococca bush in flower: it is so insignificant that we forget its existence between one winter and the next.

Mervyn puts mounds of leaf-mould round the stems of all shrubs and climbing plants in the summer garden, to nourish the roots and save some summer watering.

I cut the stems of the clematis 'Étoile Violette' down

to one foot from the ground. This hateful thing to have to do strengthens the roots of any viticella clematis. 'Étoile Violette' climbs up a vigorous 'New Dawn' rose, purple flowers harmonising well with pale pink ones.

7 February

The first frog arrives in one of the wild garden ponds. Where do frogs hide in the winter? There is frog-spawn floating about in the ponds too. Canadian pond weed, sinuous and triffid-like, has spread prolifically. Will it help suppress the algae, green and shiny, and such a scourge in summer water? We will put just one more lily in each of the four canal ponds: we like to see plenty of reflection in water, and so plant sparsely.

A daffodil is in bloom in the wild garden; like other bulbs, it is flowering late. The daffodils in this part of the garden are all the native Lent lily, small, only nine inches high, with creamy petals and yellow trumpets. Their diminutive size is a protection against wind and rain: because they are too short to be buffeted they flower bravely for four weeks or so. We have a colony of these; they are so old-fashioned as to be almost obsolete and are hard to find in any garden centre.

Tiny cobalt blue scilla have appeared in their permanent corner of the rosebed.

9 February

I have not seen Mervyn for several hours, days even, except when he arrives and leaves. So that I brave the

The veranda

cold sea wind and search until I hear voices from deep in the wood. There he and John are, happy as larks it seems, looking at me half guiltily for spending precious gardening time in the wild. They have emptied an old rubbish dump and made a charming dell, or wooded hollow, complete with romantic boulders, like a Victorian vignette. I cannot be cross: we are always trying to make pictures at Knockmore.

11 February

Shopping in Bray, our local coastal town, is desperately cold, even agonising. There is a knife-like freezing wind making furious breakers on the sea. And yet, surprisingly, the veranda is warm enough to sit in for the first time this year. A strong sun shines through the glass which the north-east wind cannot penetrate.

A surprise visitor from Scotland brings a photograph of the Mays and their nieces, beaming faces, young and middle-aged, over high-necked Edwardian blouses, having a jolly family breakfast on the veranda. In their day it was open to the air with a slate roof, and glass only on each side. The Mays being fresh air fiends, often spent warm summer nights sleeping there and used it for meals in the daytime.

About forty years ago the veranda was glassed in and became a complete, if flimsy, room, not perfect for plants because of its slate roof, but pleasant for people. Now half the room is given up to a convivial group of old wicker chairs with sun-faded covers, enjoyed by the dog and cat as well as by us. The other half is a jumble of garden things, trugs, baskets of tools, watering cans of all sizes. There are about twenty plants, all rather limp at the end of winter.

14 February

Another tempting day to spend on the sunny veranda, and rather than idle the time away, I look over the plants. We are not clever at managing container plants: until last spring they were more likely to die than live. Then we discovered that magical substance slow-release fertiliser. We pushed capsules into the potted earth and were amazed at the transformation; all the plants immediately became green and even robust, and what is more, sustained this improvement for half a year at least. There is no need to worry about the plants' present jaded look: they are waiting for April when the next capsule will renew their vitality.

Then we will enjoy the tall lemon-scented geraniums *Pelargonium graveolens* and our long-branched plumbagos, one blue-flowered and one white, and also the sturdy 'White Marseilles' fig tree. The azalea will have finished flowering and be waiting for a place outside in the shade. We have the usual cheerful muddle of small pelargoniums. None of the plants are rare, but all of them are attractive and, helped by the fertiliser capsules, easy to look after.

17 February

I bring out our first seed potatoes, choosing 'British Queen'; reasonably quick-growing and with a fine earthy flavour. We are longing to experiment with 'Rooster', smooth and red-skinned, as our main crop. Mervyn arranges the Queens in tomato boxes with eyes pointing upwards and leaves them on the veranda where next week broad beans, sown in pots, will join them.

It is good that we have a large old table on the veranda, covered with blue-checked oilcloth. There is room for many things, including a seed tray, sown with leeks. Leeks are the most rewarding of crops, growing even in winter during any warm spell. We always associate them exclusively with rainy places like Wales, but we are wrong: they were so well established, astonishingly, in ancient Egypt that bunches of leeks were part of a labourer's wage in 3000 BC. The crops must have been heavily irrigated. A wet year is a good year for leeks.

20 February

In a general tidy up, I find an article on fashionable gardens; in an old magazine it lists plants and styles that were *in* and others that were *out*. Anything written about *ins* and *outs* is an irresistible read: I am intrigued to find how Knockmore garden could be rated. Old-fashioned roses, box cones and hedges, lavender and catmint were *in*. We have all of those. Silver, mauve and generally soft colours were *in* too; we have those as well, but we mix some crimson and purple into our colour schemes.

Oh dear! We do not like lady's mantle, *Alchemilla mollis,* though there are masses of it; it was very much *in*. And our garden furniture is mostly white, very passé; it should be blueish or dark green.

Good marks were earned for banning orange flowers and for not growing conifers or heathers. These were *out*. But fashion flows on. Gravel gardens have come into vogue since the piece was written in 1992 and so have 'hot borders' and special grasses. We have the first but will probably never have the second or third.

24 February

A few chionodoxa are in bloom. My English mother used to call them glory of the snow. Since there is little snow in Ireland, they are usually called by their difficult botanical name. These pretty little flowers come from Asia Minor and are like blue and white stars. My mother scattered them over a rosebed, a round one encircled by a lavender hedge. They thrived there, but with us they survive a more dangerous existence, struggling in grass and threatened by the motor mower.

I read in *The Times* today that a landowner in England has had eight hundred young cherry trees stolen. The English, bored stiff by tasteless foreign cherries, are demanding a return to the flavoursome cherries of Merrie England. Young cherry trees are worth their weight in gold, so they need twenty-four-hour protection.

25 February

Beyond the kitchen garden beech hedge is a space with nothing in it except a large, neglected apple tree. It says much for this strain of Bramley cooker that the tree supplies us with apples for four or five months, though it is never sprayed, pruned or fertilised and the fruit is not thinned.

John and Mervyn are keen to make this space into an orchard; they say that every garden this size should have a section for hard fruit. They may be right but they are forgetting that the 'space' is in a hollow surrounded by trees, and that orchards need light, air and fresh breezes. It is madness to plant more fruit trees there but we shall risk disappointment with two early-flowering pears, 'Williams' Bon Chrétien' and 'Conference'. They should pollinate each other and bloom well even if they never bear fruit, and there are few flowers lovelier than pear blossom.

27 February

Yesterday Audrey, the rector's wife, just returned from holiday in Australia, produced a photograph of brightly-coloured birds feeding from a bird-table. The table was protected with strands of wire to keep the greedy large birds out and the little ones safe and happy. This morning Mervyn copied this contraption, making a neat cage over our own bird-table. The tits and robins find it a haven and fly in and out for birdseed all through the afternoon; they look drab compared with Australian birds but equally happy. Meanwhile the magpies sulk from neighbouring branches.

A letter from the Irish Georgian Society booking in a group at midsummer. The visiting calendar is filling up. Just now we cannot believe in midsummer, though our garden work is all a preparation for it. The wind is bitter, trees and bushes are buffeted, outdoors is an unpleasant place: February has been the ordeal it usually is. The evenings, though still cold, are brighter.

There is a pretty group of small flowers, round the root of the old deodar cedar, snowdrops, cyclamen leaves and mauve crocuses.

Recipe for February: Colcannon

Every family has its version of this traditional Irish dish. Some people make it with raw onion and cabbage or kale. We make it with leeks and spinach because we grow these in the garden, and find this mixture both filling and savoury—very satisfying in cold weather.

INGREDIENTS

Serves three to four

4 large potatoes, peeled
2 medium sized leeks, chopped finely
4 leaves of spinach, washed and drained
250 ml/½ pint milk
60 g/2 oz/½ stick butter
salt
freshly ground black pepper

METHOD

Steam or boil the potatoes and leeks together.

Cook the spinach: place it in a medium to large saucepan over a gentle heat. It will cook in its own moisture in one or two minutes, wilting down in the pan.

Mash the potato and leek together.

Chop the spinach well and add to the potato and leek.

Heat the milk and butter together in a small saucepan.

Add this gradually to the potato mixture and beat. Keep very hot.

Add salt and pepper to taste.

When the potato mixture is the consistency you like, serve it, piping hot, with bacon or sausages.

March

The wild garden

1 March

March has come in like a lion. Winds roar, branches
swing, waves smash on the sea front. Ferries to Holyhead
have been cancelled for today, to everyone's relief.

There are plenty of little flowers in the wild garden,
ones that have sturdy stems with blossoms below the
battering wind, celandines, snowdrops and wild daffodils; scilla and chionodoxa are in their usual corners of
the summer garden. Taller plants, hellebores and
bergenias, are in bloom in very sheltered places.

John and Mervyn have made the little bridge in the wild garden. It is the simplest possible construction: two stout planks to walk over and a railing made of coppiced hazel from the wood. The handrail arches slightly, making, at a distance, a silhouette like the bridge on a willow pattern plate. This little bridge, only crossing the merest trickle of water, brings the wild garden to life and sets off the pools, channels and mossy stones. We all think that the bridge looks settled immediately, as if it has always been there.

3 March

John and I are discussing local churchyards. Catholic churchyards are often planted so sparsely that the churches seem to rise straight out of grass and tarmac, softened with only a few lonely shrubs. Protestant churchyards, on the other hand, tend to be thick with funereal conifers, grown, unfortunately, sky high. Why not enjoy ourselves? If every churchyard in County Wicklow were planted with two or three double-white cherry trees, *Prunus avium* 'Plena', the blossom would lift the landscape at Easter, cheering us up after the dreary winter. Cherries are easy to maintain. Because of the vivid red of their leaves in autumn, the trees are as beautiful then as they are in spring. How splendid it would be if County Wicklow, where both wild and cultivated cherry trees grow so well, were one day famous for blossom-filled churchyards. This would enhance the county's claim to be the garden of Ireland.

6 March

A peaceful afternoon cleaning the little tombstones in the pets' graveyard with sandpaper. We have planted a carpet of minor periwinkle to show up the five pretty headstones. We think that the pets were all dogs; the Mays loved their dogs so much that they read a burial service over them in this secluded corner of the wild garden. All their staff, inside and out, attended the little ceremony. We can picture the small procession. First would come the head gardener wheeling the dog in a barrow, then the two Miss Mays, one carrying a prayerbook; after them would walk the two other gardeners, the housemaid and Mary the cook. Prayers would be said over the new grave.

These are the inscriptions:

First Stone: *Flirt died 1887*
  Dear Trusty died 1940

Second Stone: *Bur a friend for 16 years 1903.*

Third Stone: *Colleen Merrill 1900–1913*
  Danny, loving and beloved 1904–1920
  Arivederci

Fourth Stone: *Dear Duchess 1921–1936*
  Dear Lassie 1925–1936

Fifth Stone: *VIP Beta 19 years*

7 March

We have a letter this morning about the group of Swiss rose-growers; they would like to see the garden at the end of June, luckily, peak time for nearly all our roses. There will be forty-five of them. The Swiss have just discovered Ireland, writes the travel agent, and are queuing up to come here: we must be welcoming to these surely model tourists. Mervyn volunteers to come and help with our difficult entrance, even though the group is booked for nine-thirty on a Sunday morning. Because of a bad corner outside our gates, buses have to stop on the other side of the road and visitors are then escorted across.

The wind is bitter and outside work not tempting, but we are buoyed up by the anticipation of visiting the gardens of Nice and Menton for nine days from 20 March: it is a wonderful way to shorten the winter. Before we go, we must prune all the hydrangeas, the two variegated buddleia and the four *Clematis viticella*. And the kitchen garden needs attention.

8 March

'Why do old houses in County Wicklow always face due east?' asks Charles Acton, the distinguished music critic. He and his wife are visiting us with cousins of his who had inherited this house from the Mays in 1946. Unluckily, the house had to be sold very soon afterwards because of sickness in the family. All our visitors remember the place well and feel nostalgic.

'Houses faced east because everyone wanted a view of the sea', I volunteer, 'and because there was a tradition that the south wind brought tuberculosis.'

Charles remembers the cold of that fine east-facing house Kilmacurragh in south Wicklow, famous for its arboretum, where he spent part of his childhood. Two of his uncles died there of tuberculosis, perhaps because of the murderous east wind. We are so vulnerable to this wind that from January to May we abandon our front, east-facing rooms, calling them the Arctic zone. The plants in the narrow front borders suffer, having nothing like the vigour of those in more sheltered places. Rough sea surf, cupped by folding hills, looks picturesque from the front door, but in the winter and early spring the sea wind is an enemy.

11 March

We are having the last gulp of our breakfast tea when Mervyn comes in looking like a stoic who has had bad news. 'The terraces are down', he says. We hurry outside and there they are, or a large part of them, demolished as if by a bomb, but in fact destroyed by water from behind.

We are especially fond of the terraces. They support the high walk, and for our first twenty-five years here they were buried under scrub and bramble. Five years ago Mervyn started to excavate, finding warm stone and carefully made contours. I have always loved dry-wall gardens and revelled in stocking this readymade one

The dark walk

with rock pinks, creeping gypsophila and other sunlovers. Last summer the plants were already attracting countless bees and butterflies.

Before June, when our first groups are due to arrive, the terraces must be rebuilt; this autumn they must be replanted.

12 March

It is a good day because of the most beautiful spring weather. Suddenly the sun shines and the wind drops: the birds sing for the whole morning. I pick ten Algerian irises, white ones, from the sunny cottage border. Blue Apennine anemones help to make the wild garden a dream of blue, golden yellow (celandines) and white (wood anemones). All these, sprinkled over the short grass, are revelling in the sunshine.

There is a little *Magnolia stellata* beside the gravel garden. A few flowers are starting to break through their furry winter buds, as they are on the large *Magnolia denudata* in the summer garden. Before long, there will be at least a thousand blooms on the bigger tree, magnificent unless a sharp frost turns every flower jet black in a single night. This has happened in some springs, making us threaten to cut the tree down, a threat we have never had the nerve to carry out.

15 March

I stand in the sunny wild garden, admiring the blue Appenine anemones and thinking about William Robinson. He was an Irish gardener of forceful character who challenged the whole gardening establishment in these islands and ultimately much of the world. Growing up in mid-Victorian times, when gardening was mainly rigid bedding out and second-class ornaments, Robinson loved to nurture plants, both wild and cultivated, for their own sakes. Almost single-handedly he converted most of the gardening world to natural planting, over long years of vivid writing in books and magazines.

In his best-selling *The Wild Garden*, published in 1870, he wrote: 'As for the blue anemone, it is simply one of the loveliest spring flowers of any clime and should be in every garden. . . .' Charlotte and Stella May, well-read women, must have known Robinson's book, because the wild garden at Knockmore is full of these pretty flowers. Robinson also mentioned primroses, violets and bluebells for the late spring, and afterwards Welsh poppies, foxgloves, willow herb and autumn crocus. All these grow in the wild garden.

18 March

We have a telephone call this morning from the chairwoman of a County Meath gardening club wishing to arrange a group visit in May. Luckily, John manages to persuade her to change the date to mid-June when the roses and herbaceous plants will be starting to flower. May is between seasons at Knockmore, all long grass and dead daffodils. The shrubs we have planted to improve the garden at this time of year are still too small to make an impression.

19 March

We have finished all the spring pruning. Before leaving for our annual holiday in the south of France, we check the kitchen garden. Early potatoes and broad beans, germinated on the veranda, have been planted out. We are still picking Swiss chard and leeks. Asparagus kale, now that it is netted against woodpigeons, will be ready for our return, when we will enjoy pale forced rhubarb and seakale. Other vegetables will be sown in April.

21 March

Not exactly escape to happiness, because happiness is probably being able to cope with our responsibilities, but escape to a different world, to no responsibilities at all, to blue skies nine days out of ten. We are at Menton on the Côte d'Azur and the first thing I notice, as always, is the vegetation: it could not be more different from our own. I see no beech, lime or oak trees, nothing deciduous, except the handsome well-pollarded planes lining Menton's streets. In the wild and in gardens there are umbrella pines, olive trees, date palms and mimosa, the flowers just finished. Orange and lemon trees, laden with fruit, are everywhere, the street orange trees admittedly dusty but still colourful. The earth near this coast is pale and dry, not dark and moist like ours. Gardening techniques must be different because growth stops for the long hot summer.

25 March

We see two beautiful gardens today, both on steeply rising ground, inevitable here where craggy hills and mountains make sheer slopes down to the Mediterranean.

Few gardens can have such a romantic setting as the famous La Mortola, just across the Italian border, a garden created nearly a hundred and fifty years ago by the Hanbury family, but now in the charge of Genoa University. Behind are the mountains, below is the sea, the cobalt sea, as the guide books call it. There are innumerable flights of steps, paths, pergolas, pools and urns all with a background of olive, palm and cedar trees. Wisteria and Banksian roses are in flower this March, plants that will not flower in Ireland until May. There is a citrus orchard, a cactus section and an important botanical collection. Somewhere in the middle is a bright pink villa, undistinguished but with dramatic views of the Mediterranean over the palm trees.

La Mortola is sumptuous, but at the same time disappointing. John likes to see an overall plan, but the maps of the garden make us dizzy. We become more and more confused as we walk along pergolas, up and down steps, onto terraces, all lavishly planted. We admire but are exhausted.

Serre de la Madone, on the French side of Menton, is a garden on a smaller scale. It is a series of richly planted terraces flanked by exotic trees and leading up to a simple yellow-washed house in the Provençal style. The garden was made between the wars by Major Lawrence Johnston of Hidcote Manor; as at Hidcote, each section is a complete outdoor room, yet the structure of the garden is visible from many points. There are no sea views, but it has an ordered beauty that is lacking at La Mortola. A young Manchester University student on secondment shows us around. He is working for the European Union, which is helping to restore this most deserving garden.

Sunburnt and thirsty after these excursions, we sink into the shade of our little hotel's courtyard. The proprietor asks if we would like lemon in our tea. Yes, we would; French tea is made so weak. He strolls to a glossy leaved bush near the wall, picks a lemon and slices it for us there and then. The clear yellow slices make the most refreshing lemon tea we have ever tasted.

30 March

We are back home to cold air, to grey skies and to everyone strangely saying how fine the weather is. We missed the people who came on Friday to collect daffodils for Kilbride Church. I could hug our damp fresh soil, but long for the blue skies and gentle breezes of spring on the Côte d'Azur. We remind ourselves that summer by the Mediterranean would be unpleasantly hot, dusty and swarming with weary tourists.

Recipe for March:
Rhubarb Compôte

We are spoilt. We only eat the forced rhubarb, sweet, pale and quick-cooking, grown under a couple of large tea chests in the kitchen garden. It makes an excellent meringue-topped pudding, but is also delicious when stewed and always improved by orange juice.

INGREDIENTS

Serves four

2 tablespoons water

125 g/¼ lb sugar, white or brown according to taste

juice of 1 orange

500 g/1 lb forced rhubarb, cut in 1 cm/½ inch pieces

METHOD

Bring the water, sugar and orange juice to the boil; simmer it gently until the sugar is dissolved, stirring constantly.

Add the rhubarb pieces and bring the mixture to simmering point again.

Young rhubarb will soften if moved off direct heat to a warm part of the stove; older fruit will need gentle simmering. Test it constantly: it easily disintegrates. The rhubarb is ready when it is tender but still holding its shape.

Serve warm with pouring cream.

April

1 April

How cold the air feels to us and how grey the skies seem. There has been no rain, making the earth dryly forbidding. Will any seeds germinate in this cold and cheerless soil? Mervyn, as always, is hopeful, and keen to start sowing beetroot and spinach. We will try cautiously with half-packets.

There is more activity in the garden. Every week from now until the autumn Jimmy will cut the grass and Sheila will tend the border plants.

The unkind weather has not killed any blossom. Three magnolias, different ones, are in flower, with at least one thousand waxy white blooms on the *Magnolia denudata*. Flowers on the two viburnums are looking pretty and smelling sweet and our boundary walls of wild cherry are 'hung with snow' like the ones in A.E. Housman's famous poem. We sometimes think of opening the garden when all the wild cherries are flowering;

it is a wonderful sight. But the blossoms, unluckily, are dependent on the weather and unpredictable. Like most wild plants, the blooms are short-lived: after five days they wither.

The orderly design of Serre de la Madone in Menton, where the garden is welded into one structure seen easily from above and from below, has made us dissatisfied. Knockmore garden, made in a hollow between house and wood, had no such planning; old paths and hedges slice across the hollow, all of them undestroyable. The Miss Mays made features where and when the whim suited them, so that the long lily pond nearly collides with the double border, and the pretty box-edged rosebeds are jammed up against the kitchen garden.

Nowadays gardens are designed with focal points. We need one badly at the top of the double border, and have so far filled this space with one of our white seats; it will soon be replaced by John's steps up to the wood, much more special. And at the end of one of the summer garden lawns we have planted a whitish dogwood, *Cornus controversa* 'Variegata', to take the eye. The little bridge in the wild garden should have the same magnetism. We cannot, and would not want to, alter the structure of the Mays' garden much, but we can embellish a little.

4 April

Our seakale bed looks like the remains of a fair day, but we are starting to revel in the crop. We have eight seakale plants all needing to be forced to make the most delicious vegetable ever. And we have only one genuine forcing pot. We travelled all over the English Midlands to find this and ran it to earth in a remote Warwickshire valley. It came back in the car as a fat passenger safely held in by a seat belt. The pot cost £37, is well designed and gives its part of the bed great style; on the other hand, it is small for our seakale plants and cold too; they do not thrive inside the pot unless the sun shines. So we cover our other seven seakale plants with anything suitable from the garden sheds. The most successful coverings are big tea chests; the plants love their roomy warmth. Otherwise, we use any old buckets we can find, hideous to look at and only moderately efficient.

7 April

Down to the wild garden to find that, under the lower maple, there are wild flowers growing as prolifically as the ones we see on mediaeval tapestries like 'The Lady and the Unicorn' in the Cluny Museum, Paris. Primroses, violets and celandines are mixed thickly over the ground. We hope the celandines, so shining and pretty, do not devour the other plants; they are great spreaders.

9 April

John and I walk over the cowslip field beside the house. It is covered with flowers. I pick six bunches for the charity sale at neighbouring Killruddery where they always sell like hot cakes; their prettiness is given added glamour by the rumour of them dying out.

As well as cowslips, there are cuckoo flowers in the field. These fragile mauve-flowered plants, called by some 'lady's smock', are spreading to the front field and to the garden, wherever they can find some moist grass.

15 April

Cora found a hedgehog last night, curled up into a tight, spiky ball; she always has hysterics over hedgehogs, barking at them shrilly and even taking hold of them, but she has never succeeded in killing one, not just because we remove her but because the prickles defeat her. This one was under our great lime tree in a heap of lawn mowings. It is gone by morning, probably long before; they can move a mile in one night.

Meals are so enjoyable with our own asparagus kale, Swiss chard, leeks and, best of all, seakale. Forced rhubarb under tea chests is tender, pink and juicy. The early potato plants are showing.

16 April

A letter from Morayshire: Sandy Dunbar, great nephew of the Miss Mays, is coming to Ireland for a wedding at the end of the month. May he come to see the garden? He has the happiest of memories like all people who played here as children.

The terraces

19 April

Jimmy McCabe, smiling and ruddy-faced, is rebuilding the collapsed terraces with his son and a few skilful helpers. They have made four fine-looking dry walls, but it is a bit frustrating from a gardener's point of view. To make a well-stocked dry wall the planting should be done while the wall is being built.

We have several pretty new dry wall plants, rock pinks, and creeping gypsophila among them, all ready to plant, but Jimmy will not hear of it. Someone poking in plants while the wall is under construction would be too disturbing. He is kind but firm, like the ideal kindergarten teacher. We have to submit to planting when the wall is finished; this way many of the plants may not survive, though we shall try squeezing them into the holes with damp moss or underfelt.

23 April

The garden is full of withered daffodils. They look dreadful, make lots of work cutting off the flowering stalks and force us to put off mowing while they stand for six more weeks, and then the grass will be like wire. If we ever take over another garden, it will be a relief not to grow daffodils at all. We might have just the short wild ones or a few in a tub in a conservatory. We would concentrate outside on the early spring bulbs, small enough to be immune to the wind and the rain and to allow for May grass cutting.

24 April

An article in *The Irish Times* extols the healthgiving qualities of tomatoes. We should eat them at least ten times a week. Could we, or would we, even if we could? Luckily we grow plenty and usually have our own from early August until mid-December: we have enough to make purée as well for winter soups and stews. To achieve this long season again, we have just bedded seven tomato plants in the greenhouse, and we shall sow seeds tomorrow to take over from today's plants, when they are finished.

25 April

Jimmy McCabe, his son and helpers are hacking at the far bank to make steps up to the wood. It is tough work, but they have nearly finished. The steps will be a much-needed focal point at the end of the double border: they are simply made from old railway sleepers and the gradient is gradual. John's plan is that they will invite people to walk easily from the richly bordered central path into the dark stillness of the wood.

It seemed a mad scheme to me at first, but I now admit it is original, even magnetic, and am planning pale-coloured flowers at the woodland ends of the double border to smooth the merging of borders to wood.

26 April

We enjoy the last of the seakale; also some Swiss chard and a little forced rhubarb. And we have the leeks and asparagus kale to eat, not bad during the yearly hungry gap in soil too poor to raise any of the cabbage family. Because the ground is dry and the weather still cold, we have sown few seeds outside yet.

27 April

The steps up to the wood are finished at last, adding a new dimension to the garden. We cannot wait until June when we shall walk up the path between two billowing borders and mount the steps to a different world, quiet, dark, sheltered from the bright exhausting day. We have placed two long granite blocks on stone supports in the wood. People can sit on them in peace, looking across the Dargle Valley, imagining sleeping hedgehogs, silent birds and hidden red squirrels.

The day before yesterday the weather, dry for much too long, broke and there has been gentle rain ever since. It is depressing to listen to rain for forty-eight hours but comforting to think of it sinking down into the earth. The smaller plants look brighter already and we are happy about our shrubs. Last year we lost a handsome philadelphus and a magnificent shrub rose because of a drought the previous summer. They just withered and died. No amount of watering could revive them.

28 April

Especially fine now are the aquilegia, sometimes called columbines There is a throng of them, three hundred or more, jostling one another on the bank below the terraces. Some people would consider these to be weeds; they are obviously self-seeded from selected plants put in by the Miss Mays almost a century ago. Now they are like wild columbines, except that instead of being only purple, they graduate in many toning colours, dark pink, blue, cream or a mixture of all these. They make such a lovely picture that we are taking some to plant on the newly restored terrace beds to extend the line. The colours blend with the mellow stone of the terraces and when the flowers die, their leaves make a pretty ground cover. Not so long ago it would have been thought ridiculous to have semi-wild flowers in a garden, but fashions change and they are now accepted, even enjoyed.

30 April

Sandy Dunbar comes to see us after his family wedding. His mother, a niece of the Miss Mays, spent her holidays here during the Great War, and told Sandy about the garden, the wood and the river Dargle. She loved it all but especially liked running down to the river to bathe and to fish. Sandy himself came here as a boy in 1939 and remembers the ponds, the terraces and the dogs' graves. He hated the dogs—they nipped his bare legs—but his great aunts loved them. We tell him about the funeral services, but he had never been to one. He might have enjoyed it.

Sandy is unluckily agonised by toothache when he is here. He tells us that Phoebe Whitworth, the Mays' eldest niece, wrote interesting memoirs of her childhood in Hong Kong, Hawaii and Ireland, before the Great War, mentioning her aunts and Knockmore several times. He has promised to send us a copy. We hope he will make the journey from Morayshire to see us again, the next time without toothache.

Recipe for April:
Seakale

Seakale should be forced in the dark. Cut the shoots when they are about nine inches long and still a greenish white. They will be tender and succulent.

INGREDIENTS

Serves two

350 g/¾ lb seakale shoots
1 teaspoon salt
60 g/2 oz butter or margarine
juice of half a lemon
1 tablespoon parsley, chopped

METHOD

Plunge the seakale into boiling water and simmer it until the shoots are just tender, about 15 minutes. Drain and keep warm.

Meanwhile melt the butter at the side of the stove, add the lemon juice and parsley and pour this over the seakale.

Serve at once.

May

1 May

Suddenly we have two summer days: blue skies, scudding clouds, fresh breezes. I drive to Powerscourt Garden Centre to buy twine, seed compost and other necessities. Leaves in Powerscourt's beech avenue, already fully out, are a pale fresh green; so are the ones on the handsome lime avenue beyond the great house. Back home, our own lime tree is also in leaf and our prominent horsechestnut tree is covered with cream-coloured flowers.

4 May

The kitchen garden is starting to look dynamic, as it should. Mervyn is hard at work sowing beetroot, leeks and spinach, all this having been put off in last month's cold drought. He has made two elegant bamboo wigwams for sweet peas, traditionally planted in our kitchen garden beds. Broad beans and early potatoes are growing well. Seakale plants are tidied and settled for their summer leafmaking. Packets of runner beans and courgettes are ready to go in when the danger of frost is past.

7 May

Time was when May was zero month in this garden. No one would believe this because May is the great month for County Wicklow garden visiting. At Knockmore it seemed to be a time of tightly closed rose buds and triumphant dandelions. There was and still is an unusually large and lovely snowdrop tree, *Halesia monticola*. It is usually in flower but it is tucked away. We carried on happily with this state of affairs for some years, telling ourselves that May gave us a much needed rest, and that not every garden could be a rhododendron paradise until, one May a few years ago, we had a telephone call: 'May I bring a dozen visitors to you this afternoon?' asked a distinguished garden writer. We protested that there was absolutely nothing in flower. But they came nonetheless and were entirely delightful, all from New England and all sensibly dressed in raincoats and boots. We were not to apologise for no flowers; they were gardeners so they understood.

Because there were no flowers, our visitors noticed other things. 'Oh my! such a cute little sundial!' one of them said, and she was right. We have never seen a sundial like it, nor can we find a picture resembling our sundial in any book. It was in pieces when we came here, lost under broken flowerpots in a laurel arbour. We mended it, set the dial to give Greenwich time and put it all back on its brick platform, halfway down the grass in the summer garden. It looks lonely there: sundials should be surrounded not by grass, but by sun-loving plants like lavender. Yet none would survive in that frost pocket. The pedestal is elegant, the dial not flat like other dials but formed from two wing-like shapes. From some angles the dial looks like a bird taking flight. All the best sundials have an inscription, preferably in Latin. Ours is nearly obliterated but we can still make it out:

> Serenus dies   Serenus sit animus
> Hic me posuerunt Phoebe et Stella*

Phoebe, author of memoirs, and Stella were sisters, two of the Mays' many nieces. The sundial was set up, we think, before the Great War to commemorate a happy summer they had spent at Knockmore. Did the children's father, Sir Henry May, Governor of Hong Kong or did their aunts, plan this charming memento? We shall never know.

10 May

We were ashamed that those pleasant visitors had seen no flowers in May, so the following autumn we stocked up with May-flowering shrubs. Now in May we enjoy *Solanum crispum, Rubus* x *tridel* 'Benenden', *Abutilon*

---

* Bright days, calm souls.
  Phoebe and Stella placed me here

vitifolium, a fremontodendron, a deutzia and two mag-nolias, *M. liliiflora* and *M. wilsonii.* All flourish. The solanum and the abutilon give us blue flowers, the rubus, deutzia and *M. wilsonii* white ones and the flowers of *M. liliiflora* are a rich purple.

12 May

It is extraordinary how often hedgehogs make news. There is a piece about them in today's *Irish Times.* Hun-dreds of them woke up a month ago and were killed by the cold drought, and by the lack of their favourite food, slugs and worms, which stayed hidden away. There is one here tonight, one that is very much alive, and curls up in time to protect itself from Cora, the scourge of all hedgehogs. John makes her sit beside this one without tormenting it—a great achievement. We hope it will escape down into the fern, grass and laurels of the Dargle Valley.

13 May

Since yesterday we have the name of the house engraved on our gate pillar, something I thought that no one ever did in the country. Enniskerry, though, is no longer country: more and more houses are inserted into every crevice and there are at least two expensive suburban developments within a mile of us. Gardaí, ambulance men, postmen, couriers and many others who have been losing their way to us for years will be relieved to see KNOCKMORE carved out of the granite. The capitals, filled in delicately with black paint on the rough granite, look as if the name had been there for a century.

16 May

The month is looking more promising in spite of the burden of weeds and grass growing relentlessly. The transparency of young leaves is, as always, like a miracle after all the long cold months of bare branches: young leaves on the beech hedges have pushed off last year's brown foliage, suddenly making these the prettiest hedges in the garden.

Little Alpine plants are flowering on the rockery, many of them the wild Burren geranium and Alpine strawberry. They have never been arranged in any way by us and look as if they were just sprinkled indiscriminately over the steep slopes. Sometimes we try to organise the rockery into blocks or rivers of colour but find this extraordinarily difficult. Then we tell ourselves that we like it better as a chaotic sprinkle.

A few roses have started to bloom very early: 'Penelope', 'Souvenir de Saint Anne's' and 'Scabrosa'. Apart from them, the garden is full of tightly closed buds, promising a prolific season. A garden in waiting.

18 May

Abutilon vitifolium is in full flower. Without any doubt it is the prettiest tree in the whole garden, with its vine-like evergreen leaves and pale blue flower clusters. Every year we wonder if our abutilon will survive the winter: we have had to replace our first plant three or four times. Our present abutilon is tucked cosily behind a solid buddleia 'Harlequin' and is against the west wall of the house, a warm position, but even so the leaves look withered with cold in February and March. Luckily the tree recovers in April, forms larger green leaves in early May and flowers abundantly before the end of the month.

It was a pleasure to discover from W. J. Bean's *Trees and Shrubs Hardy in the British Isles* that the *Abutilon vitifolium*, a Chilean plant, was introduced to these islands in the 1830s by a Captain Cottingham of Dublin, an enterprising plantsman living near Glasnevin and the Botanic Gardens, where he had many contacts. The tree is so lovely that several English visitors last year saw it and planted one back home. We doubt if any will survive the cold English winter.

21 May

We have just thrown out our wild irises, a bitter disappointment. Several years ago Con, who helped us then, brought some to us from Enniskerry's Bog Meadow. The plants seemed to flourish by the ponds. After a few years, though, we realised that they had not produced a single flower and probably never would: too much shade, perhaps. This was sad because the handsome *Iris pseudacorus*, large and yellow, was so popular beside Irish rivers a hundred years ago that people decorated their houses with bunches of the flowers for the Corpus Christi procession in June. And the plants have a legendary history in France; Clovis, King of the Franks, made the yellow iris an emblem of France after a group of them had shown him where he could escape from the Goths across a river. This was in the sixth century. Many years later the flowers were called 'fleur de Louis', after French kings, then 'fleur de lys', the royal heraldic device. In old English books the iris is 'flower de Luce'.

So the poor irises had to go onto the rubbish heap, or rather 'the eternal flame' as the family call it. All spring, summer and autumn, on every windless day, the garden rubbish is slowly burning. Otherwise the heap would be as large as a cottage within a week. The thin column of smoke rising from it is part of the garden landscape, and the ash is put carefully round rose and soft fruit bushes. John is especially fond of tending

The gravel garden

the eternal flame. Why do men enjoy making bonfires? Can it be a reversion to our cave dwelling ancestors?

24 May

When we made one, we thought it so original to have a gravel garden. It was not! We were just a tiny part of an epidemic of gravel gardens, set in motion perhaps by Beth Chatto's famous dry garden near Colchester. There are now gravel gardens described and photographed in most of the current gardening magazines and books, especially the expensive ones.

Our gravel garden started off as a Mediterranean garden, because the small, sunny triangle it occupies on the south side of the house reminded us of Italy: we had already put four eighteenth-century Roman pillars there. We began with Italian plants, *Convolvulus cneorum* and *Teucrium fruticans*, but then lapsed into using any sun-loving plant that we liked. Many of them rolled from narrow borders onto the gravel, liking the warm stones, and this was the start of the gravel garden.

Now, looking at it out of the winter room window, we can see silvery lambs' tongues, pale rock roses, wild strawberries and apple mint surging onto the gravel where they have taken root. All we have planted into the gravel itself are several stork's bill geraniums, *Erodium macradenum*: they flourish and look like pretty cushions, grey and pink among the stones. We should like some more of these filigree-leaved plants, but they are hard to track down.

26 May

I watch Mervyn weeding carefully round the wild garden ponds. They look so pretty, surrounded by mossy boulders and by a mixture of wild and garden flowers. The wild flowers are frail Welsh poppies, wild strawberries, aquilegia and foxgloves, all self-seeded; garden flowers mingling well with these are bergenia and day lilies. Brooklime, a blue-flowered native plant, looking like watercress, is growing in two of the shallower ponds. It is happiest in about two inches of water.

28 May

This evening when we walk down to the wild garden we pick two newts out of the mud in the highest pond. One of them is drab, the other, the male, is well-crested with a brightly coloured tail; it is like a tiny flamboyant dragon. They are the first newts we have seen this year but have probably been living in the pond's soft mud for some time. Creatures of habit, they come back to the same pond always, making it likely that it has been the newts' pond since it was dug eighty or so years ago. Where do these little creatures hibernate? Can they live in the pond mud all winter?

30 May

I spend a horrid twenty minutes spraying the roses. It is idiotic to be afraid to use chemicals. Mervyn made the mixture up for me so I cannot avoid using it without seeming cowardly.

31 May

May was, as usual, a hard month at Knockmore. The weather was erratic, the weeds grew thick and fast, and the wild garden grass looked unpleasantly long and coarse: Jimmy will cut it with difficulty in early June. There have been, though, three glimpses of real beauty.

The first was one morning early in the month when the sun shone through the pale transparency of early beech leaves into the dim ground of the wood. The next was last week: our rampant purple geranium enhanced the pale blue flower clusters of the abutilon towering behind; both of them were set off by silvery lambs' tongues below. Then yesterday in the wild garden I noticed thirty or so foxgloves glimmering out of a cave-like recess among the trees. Sometimes foxgloves appear in impossible places, but these could not have found a more beautiful setting.

Recipe for May:
Gooseberry Tartlets

Early gooseberries can be in the shops in May. They taste best with rich, crumbly pastry.

INGREDIENTS
Makes eight small tarts

The Pastry
300 g/10 oz plain white/all purpose flour
180 g/6 oz/1½ sticks margarine or butter
60 g/2 oz caster sugar
2 egg yolks
a little water

The Filling
240 g/½ lb gooseberries
120 g/4 oz brown sugar (Demerara)

METHOD
Cut the margarine or butter into small pieces and mix into the flour with a knife. Then rub with your finger tips until the mixture is like breadcrumbs.

Add the caster sugar and mix in well.

Beat the egg yolks, extending them with a very little

water. Add this to the mixture to make a soft dough. Knead the dough lightly with floury hands on a floured surface.

Wrap the pastry in clingfilm and leave it to rest in the fridge for about half an hour. Meanwhile, top and tail the gooseberries and sugar them well..

Preheat the oven to gas mark 6/400°F/200°C.

Roll the pastry out very gently, giving it a half turn at intervals. Use a floury pastry board and rolling pin.

Reserve a quarter of the pastry for the lattice effect. Stamp out rounds on the large piece of rolled pastry: they should fit patty tins.

Line each patty tin with a pastry round and then fill with some well sugared gooseberries. Cut strips of pastry and make lattice work across the top of the tartlets.

Brush over with cold water and a little caster sugar and bake for 20 minutes. Then put damp tinfoil over and finish at gas mark 5/375°F/190°C to soften the gooseberries.

Sprinkle with sugar. Serve hot with cream.

June

1 June

June! This month is the climax of our year. There are four groups of visitors coming to the garden when the roses peak, around midsummer. We must brace ourselves for hard work. John is a stickler for neat hedges and edges; I concentrate on the plants. We both like showing people round, telling them the history of the garden, and how we run it as a team.

The roses will flower early this year. They are all in naturally blending colours, making it a pleasure to look along the little box-edged borders and see deep red, dark pink, pale pink and white flowers merging happily. And the groups of crimson *Rosa gallica officinalis* bring the double border to life. A few of the roses, 'Souvenir de Saint Anne's', 'Cornelia', 'Penelope' and 'Buff Beauty', flower again in a subdued fashion in late August. The others, the Gallica, Alba and Spinosissima, are over by mid July. We love them all but especially those that have such a short season. The long days of midsummer are made especially magical by the scent of these velvety flowers.

6 June

There are a dozen leeks running to seed in the overflow vegetable garden above the greenhouse. It is my fault. I have been selfish about the leeks, eking them out and giving none away. They are now hard and dry, a punishment for my unchristian behaviour. Broad beans are the only new season's crop in the garden so far.

9 June

We are unhappy about our vegetables. Our three rows of dwarf beans, black, green and yellow podded respectively, are undersized alike rows of badly nourished children. They are well cared for but hate the recent unpredictable weather. We hope that the ornamental yellow courgettes, planted out this morning, will thrive better. The dark green courgettes, destined to grow into marrows, look sturdy and the reddish lettuce has germinated well.

12 June

Mervyn is bringing our four garden seats outside. None of us have time to enjoy them, but since visitors do sit on them, we like them to be on display in summer. Or rather we did until I read that article in *Gardens Illustrated* on the subject of garden seats: white is vile except in the tropics, it ran; seats should be grey, green or slate blue. I immediately had a Pauline conversion and hated our dazzling white seats. How right this dogmatic young author was! He must be young to be so very sure. I tried in vain to persuade John and Mervyn to paint the seats a soft merging colour, but No! They actually like white seats; even after reading the article. I notice, humiliated, that gardens in the glossiest magazines and gardening books all have seats in soft blues and greens or else, like Rosemary's, in plain cedar wood. Our seats will seem brash to the sophisticated.

13 June

A young man comes to the front door asking to look at our fields for a possible film scene. It is to be a duel from an unpublished work by Robert Louis Stevenson. We are sorry that our fields are not as he wished; they are too sloping. There is no open glade in a wood for duellists, flanked by their seconds, to exchange shots at dawn. The man drives away to the Phoenix Park, a more hopeful place for the rendezvous.

Why are we sorry? Why do we think shots at dawn and a duel in the field would be fun when duelling even in 1728, the date of the story, was undoubtedly a tragedy for all concerned? The tragedy seems less from this distance in time perhaps.

14 June

I am full of anxiety. For nearly a week we have had torrential rains, floods, strong winds, everything to give the plants a battering. And our first group comes in four days. I am determined to rescue as many plants as possible and am soaked to the skin after dead-heading the hybrid musk rose, 'Buff Beauty', this morning. Saving the buds and discarding the wet dead heads takes me an hour and a quarter.

16 June

The rain stopped, I work in the little rosebeds, preparing bushes for the visitors. There I think not of the Miss Mays but of my mother, who also had a little rose garden with small formal hedges. Her hedges were not of box, like ours, but of lavender, and her bushes were all pink cluster roses, I remember.

Thinking of her pretty garden, now built over, gives me dark feelings about mortality, beauty passing and the pathetically short life of any garden. I am only partly cheered by recalling that three of my mother's children inherited her passion for plants and hoping that this passion may continue down the generations when our gardens are not even a memory.

18 June

Thirty members of the Kells Garden Club come today. Some of the visitors are knowledgeable, others are just happy to walk round the garden and the wood. The roses, herbaceous plants and wild clumps are in great form: all of us, Mervyn and Sheila especially, had worked hard rescuing casualties after the rain.

The group love the roses. The most splendid sight at the moment is the climbing rose 'Rambling Rector':

Rosa spinosissima 'William III'

it throws a vast white canopy over an unfortunate apple tree called 'Blood of the Boyne'. The translucent pink 'Céleste' is flowering between two crimson to purple roses, 'Rose de Resht' and 'Cardinal Richelieu'; the contrast is thrilling yet does not clash. The visitors are especially taken with an unusual little *Rosa spinosissima* : 'William III'; it is about the size of a walnut, a mauve pink colour and the petals never quite unfurl.

One of the group introduces herself as a great niece of the Miss Mays. She is excited to revisit the garden she remembered and of which her mother had told her so much. I point out the apple loft where her mother had spent happy summer nights, half-sleeping and half-listening to her aunts' pony chomping in the stable below. She is a cousin of Sandy Dunbar, who came in April. Our visitor wonders where Charlotte May's private walk to the village of Enniskerry was: it is said in the family that Miss May still walks there.

The roses, herbaceous plants and wild garden plants are at their best for the people from Kells, but the kitchen garden is sparse, to my shame, until I learn that seeds have been disappointing for everyone this year. As I thought, the cold soil is to blame, and the wet June. Next year we must all start our rows of leeks, spinach and runner beans under cloches.

20 June

Tomorrow morning a group from Castleknock is coming and today rain is pelting down and has been for five or six hours. There are streams of water flowing down our avenue, pools lying round the house and we worry about cracks on the terrace for fear of landslides. The double border is like a battlefield strewn with corpses of pretty peach-leaved campanula; we dread seeing the bruised and sodden roses. Gentle rain is life-giving, but torrential rain is only destructive; though today is nearly the longest day, we have had to switch on lights at seventhirty and make a roaring fire to stop us looking despairingly out of the window.

21 June

Midsummer! It rains almost incessantly. This does not deter a group of forty, some of them elderly and not very mobile, from coming to see the garden. A few give up halfway and go to sit damply in their bus. The others trudge round heroically, exclaiming at the 'Rambling Rector's' white canopy, writing notes about other flowers and discussing the pruning of vines. Garden visiting is not enjoyable on a wet day in Ireland, or indeed anywhere. This group try to enjoy themselves, try very hard, but if only the sun would shine!

25 June

A charming young woman from a Dublin travel agency is here. She is enthusiastic about the garden and about our house too. Will we welcome small élite groups of Americans to see the garden and then have drinks in the house? she asks. We might in the garden's best months, mid-June to mid-September. Will we then have some to a lunch party? We are cautious this time. Her final suggestion, that we let the house to film-makers, is greeted with horror.

27 June

Listening avidly to the long-range weather forecasts, we become as obsessed about weather as any farmer or yachtsman. This is because tomorrow at ten-thirty a group from the Irish Georgian Society is coming and the next morning the group of forty-five Swiss rose-growers arrive at nine-thirty. Last evening large hail-stones clattered down the winter room chimney and today there is a bitter north wind. Another trial is that I fell and broke a rib yesterday: more than half an hour's activity is torture.

28 June

Just now I am looking out of the veranda door across streams of rain to the garden's backdrop, our row of wild cherry trees. Under the trees are John and Mervyn talking to a crowd of umbrellas. Under the umbrellas are thirty or so members of the Irish Georgian Society, trying valiantly to keep dry, warm and interested. Thank goodness, I think at a tangent, that all umbrellas are no longer black; black umbrellas make any joint venture into the rain look like a funeral procession.

In spite of the colourful umbrellas, the poor members are a distressful sight as they speed down the avenue to their bus with no time to say more than 'thank you, it must be a lovely garden in fine weather.' It was a sad repetition of Midsummer's Day. We must not be sorry for ourselves just because of two wet visiting days. Wimbledon has been a washout, a golf tournament near Paris was flooded and Lake Como has burst its banks.

29 June

The Swiss people arrive at nine-thirty this morning. Everything is right for them. The sun shines, the grass, after all the rain, is a brilliant green, the masses of *Rosa gallica* in the double border are the richest crimson imaginable and are complemented by silvery lambs' tongues and blue campanula. The Swiss are ecstatic about our border colours, the wood, the gesture of a bridge, the pets' cemetery. We realise that the patina of age and tradition does much for this garden: the mature beech hedges, the mossy stones in the wild garden, and the fern-bordered dark walk.

The group call Knockmore a lived-in garden and like it that way. Mervyn's kindly help at our entrance gates, John's excursion with them through the wood, Cora frisking round their heels and even me, leaning out of the veranda apologising for my broken rib—they respond to all these things. They give us a pretty paper stamp of a rose to remember their visit.

30 June

This is the day to sum up the month's activity. Although it has been the wettest June for fifteen years, two of the four groups struck fine days. We feel absurdly guilty about those who braved the rain, and we feel flat too, as if we have staged-managed a play that has flopped. All our visitors were most friendly and we hope they will come back. June has been as rewarding a month as we could make it.

talking to a crowd of umbrellas. Under the umbrellas are thirty or so members of the Irish Georgian Society, trying valiantly to keep dry, warm and interested. Thank goodness, I think at a tangent, that all umbrellas are no longer black; black umbrellas make any joint venture into the rain look like a funeral procession.

In spite of the colourful umbrellas, the poor members are a distressful sight as they speed down the avenue to their bus with no time to say more than 'thank you, it must be a lovely garden in fine weather.' It was a sad repetition of Midsummer's Day. We must not be sorry for ourselves just because of two wet visiting days. Wimbledon has been a washout, a golf tournament near Paris was flooded and Lake Como has burst its banks.

29 June

The Swiss people arrive at nine-thirty this morning. Everything is right for them. The sun shines, the grass, after all the rain, is a brilliant green, the masses of *Rosa gallica* in the double border are the richest crimson imaginable and are complemented by silvery lambs' tongues and blue campanula. The Swiss are ecstatic about our border colours, the wood, the gesture of a bridge, the pets' cemetery. We realise that the patina of age and tradition does much for this garden: the mature beech hedges, the mossy stones in the wild garden, and the fern-bordered dark walk.

The group call Knockmore a lived-in garden and like it that way. Mervyn's kindly help at our entrance gates, John's excursion with them through the wood, Cora frisking round their heels and even me, leaning out of the veranda apologising for my broken rib—they respond to all these things. They give us a pretty paper stamp of a rose to remember their visit.

30 June

This is the day to sum up the month's activity. Although it has been the wettest June for fifteen years, two of the four groups struck fine days. We feel absurdly guilty about those who braved the rain, and we feel flat too, as if we have staged-managed a play that has flopped. All our visitors were most friendly and we hope they will come back. June has been as rewarding a month as we could make it.

Recipe for June:
Broad Beans and Bacon

Broad beans taste best when the beans are not much larger than peas, and are a fresh green colour. They have an affinity with bacon.

INGREDIENTS
Serves two
4 rashers of short back bacon
360 g/¾ lb broad beans, shelled
1 tablespoon marjoram

METHOD
Chop the rashers into dice size pieces and fry them in a dry frying pan until they are crisp. Put them in a warm place.

Boil the broad beans in a little water until they are tender, only about five minutes, strain the water away and add the crisp rasher pieces.

Sprinkle on the marjoram.

Put the beans into a warm dish and serve at once.

Some diced bread can be fried in the bacon fat and served separately.

July

The herbaceous borders

1 July

We have no groups booked to see the garden this month; they hardly ever come in July. We do not know the reason for this. It means that we can enjoy the garden without too much stress. But it is sad that people should miss July here. Many roses are still blooming and the herbaceous perennials in the summer garden come into their own.

The groups of *Rosa gallica officinalis* will be flowering on the double border for most of the month if we cut the deadheads back carefully. This beautiful rose has many names: 'Apothecary's Rose', 'Provins Rose' and even 'Red Rose of Lancaster'. Its history is described by the great rose expert Graham Stuart Thomas as 'lost in the mists of time'. This antiquity has great attraction for me. Some people find the petals' strong magenta colour too strident. We love it and treat it with respect since it won us a first prize in the Royal Irish Horticultural Society's rose show some years ago.

3 July

I am looking at the soft fruit garden because this is the month for picking and preserving. Our first raspberries are already ripe and sweet. The red and white currant bushes throve in this year's rainy June; their fruit hangs in shining clusters. But the vegetable section of this garden makes a different picture; in every bed, seeds are still struggling to survive in the cold soil. Last year we picked runner beans early in July; this year we shall cheer if they ripen in September. The bees have been cold lately too and have stayed in their warm hives instead of foraging around in flowers. Honey will be scarce for a long time.

5 July

Hong Kong is frequently in the news. I was skimming through an account of former governors when my eye was caught by a report from the year 1912.

Sir Henry May and his wife were being carried through the streets on a sedan chair after arriving, when an assailant dashed from the crowd with a gun. The bullet missed the Governor and lodged in his wife's chair.

Sir Henry May must have known Knockmore well, and his four daughters spent many happy school holidays with their aunts. In return, the Miss Mays went on the long voyage to visit their brother in the Far East where they were attracted by all things Chinese. When we bought the house, we had a glimpse of the colourful ceramic Chinese elephants they had brought back to Ireland, but never saw the green dragons they chose to adorn the veranda roof.

8 July

In spite of my broken rib, I manage to thin three bunches of our 'Muscat of Alexandria' grapes this morning. There are still seven bunches to work on; Mervyn and I will thin them out in a day or two. This is tricky and must never be left too late since the fruit swells rapidly and can become painfully congested in a few hours, or so it seems. We nip off the fruit on the inside of the hanks, hoping that we have made enough space. This way the bunch should have good shoulders and be as handsome to look at as the grapes are delicious. Because the weather is warmer we have, at last, sown our fennel seeds. This late sowing will probably prevent the plants from running to seed, but will they mature before late August?

11 July

I am in Rosemary's kitchen garden this afternoon admiring an exceptionally tall row of peas. 'You will never guess where they came from,' she says. 'Tutankhamun's tomb.' Who could have guessed?

One of Rosemary's relatives took part in the tomb's discovery, a thrilling adventure. He was given a few of the two thousand-year-old pea seeds buried with Tutankhamun. Rosemary's family kept the strain going and here are some of them, so fresh and green! 'They taste the same as modern peas,' she says. 'The only difference is the height of the plant, eighteen inches taller than our own. Taller plants give you many more peas of course.'

15 July

Since we are invited out to lunch, there is time to look at the garden properly, though not to work in it. Flowers are blooming in the double border; from each end it looks rhythmical. Miss Jekyll, pioneer of the herbaceous border, insisted on rhythm, meaning that there should not be too many varieties of plant in a border, and that drifts of plants should be repeated several times. She used acanthus to give rhythmical structure every now and then; we use bergenia and stachys. On the whole the colours are still good: silver stachys, dark and light blue campanula, crimson roses, pale yellow thalictrum and greenish-white astrantia. Two plants spoil the effect: an orange day lily and a scarlet crocosmia; we have dug them up dozens of times but they are indestructible. If any groups come, we must remember to cut off the flowers.

17 July

It is sweet pea time. We saved our sweet pea seeds last year and this year they have germinated well; supplemented by some white-flowered ones I bought, we should have an attractive mixture. The white-flowered sweet peas were harder to germinate, but they were worth the trouble. The blooms were especially ethereal. Nearly every day I cut some of these fragrant flowers for ourselves or for friends; they are put in simple glass jars where they helpfully arrange themselves. I pick three bunches today.

Mervyn brings a basket of white currants into the kitchen. I rinse them, simmer them on the Rayburn cooker and now the juice is dripping through an old pillowcase into our mixing bowl. Tomorrow I shall make white currant jelly.

18 July

This morning I make six pots of white currant jelly. Why does it become a reddish colour, I wonder? The jelly is pretty and translucent and the flavour delicious.

This afternoon is idyllic in the summer garden: the lavender beds are alive with bees and butterflies; even the grass is warm, yet there is a fresh breeze. Some friends

The greenhouse

are here with their two-year-old child whose father tries
to interest her in the lily ponds' wriggling tadpoles and
flashing dragonflies, but she stolidly prefers to clutch
hot dry handfuls of mown grass and to throw them on
the ground.

22 July

We have a family wedding at the end of the week entailing much hoeing, weeding and edging of the avenue and sweep to give us a respectable shop front; the rest of the garden is so much more interesting that we are apt to neglect the approach. There will be seven people in the house for several days, their ages running from eighty-five down to seven. This will leave little time for gardening.

23 July

Bliss it is not in this dawn to be alive! We all feel dead in the intensely humid heat. Everywhere looks gloomy too. Clouds are darkly threatening, yet the longed for rain never comes. Leaves are dull, and recesses between the branches black. To provide for tomorrow's guests, I drag myself down to the soft fruit garden, and pick raspberries and red currants for a seasonal summer pudding. It is now sitting in a bowl in the refrigerator, firmly pressed down by a kitchen weight to soak the juice through the bread.

25 July

Our daughters' families from England and from Canada have arrived and do not find today's heat oppressive as we do. They find Ireland cool, as always.

I notice a bank beyond the kitchen garden filled with a mixture of flowers that have seeded themselves: honesty and aquilegias have come in from the garden, herb

Robert, herb Bennet and lesser willow herb from the wild. The effect is prettier than most plantings are. Everyone enjoys the summer pudding.

26 July

The wedding of our grandaughter Rebecca. After the ecumenical ceremony in St Patrick's Cathedral, the guests go to her parents' garden where they stroll and chat before and after dinner. The garden is not sloping like this one, the grass, flat as a billiard table, is bordered loosely by shrubs and old trees, giving a relaxed and charming effect. Blue-flowered solanum, fruiting pear and late-flowering roses clothe the long house wall. The evening is fine after rain; the perfect moment to enjoy a garden.

27 July

We are all happily tired after the wedding party feast and disco. This afternoon one of the family sleeps for three hours on the drawing-room sofa, another sleeps too, upstairs, and a third curls up with a detective story. John is busy hammering at a do-it-yourself wine rack and I attack the spent branches on a prickly Grootendorst rose. How lucky that we have enough space to do our own thing on a sleepy Sunday afternoon.

30 July

It is a thrill, early this morning, to find the first flowers on our blue plumbago. We forget the ethereal quality of these flowers: they are a pale yet intense blue like a reflection of blue sky. Our plant is happy on the veranda. The redoubtable plantswoman Gertrude Jekyll, helped by her nine gardeners of course, put plants of plumbago at intervals through her late summer borders.

Sheila is here this morning speaking warmly of a little 'green garden' she has seen stocked with 'lady's mantle' and box and I do not know what else. Immediately Andrew Marvell's 'green thought in a green shade' seems alluring. I have a daydream about making a green garden out of one of the Mays' small rectangular lawns. I even look up Miss Jekyll's book *Colour in the Flower Garden* to find greenish plants. A picture forms of a dark green arbour, covered with pale clematis and anchored on each side by bold acanthus or green-flowered hydrangeas, some paving too, with epimedium and apple mint flopping over it. The scheme is rejected: too expensive to make the garden, too much work to maintain it, also, as John says, the garden is so very, very green already.

31 July

Mervyn and I attack two difficult climbing roses, 'Adélaïde d'Orléans' and 'Betty Hussey'. The French rose, spectacular with hanging clusters in the summer, is now a wild mesh of skinny branches, and 'Betty Hussey' has pretty flowers but over-vigorous 'Kiftsgate' qualities: any rose with a strain of 'Kiftsgate' becomes rampant. It is a relief to know they are pruned and tied up ready for next summer.

The roses and herbaceous plants have bloomed well this July. Our favourite campanula, the pale lactiflora, never seed here, even though authoritative books tell us that they should. They loom over the border like a pale blue cloud. We have three groups and long for more. The red and white currants are prolific and the raspberries ripen on sunny days. The vegetables are still retarded by cold soil.

The lily ponds, seen through the arched trellis

Recipe for July:
Summer Pudding

This traditional recipe gives us the whole essence of a summer garden. We make two or three summer puddings and look forward to them impatiently. A litre/one and a half pint pudding bowl is needed.

Ingredients

Serves four

1 kg/2 lbs fruit—a mixture of raspberries and red-currants—120 g/4 oz of blackcurrants can be included

180 g/6 oz sugar

about 8 slices of white bread, depending on the size, crusts removed

Method

String the red currants and black currants. Rinse them quickly. Put the currants in a large saucepan with the sugar. Add the raspberries. Cook very gently until the fruit is soft and broken up.

Line the pudding bowl with slices of white bread; this is easier if the bread is cut into fingers.

Lift some of the cooked fruit out of the saucepan with a slotted spoon and put it halfway up the lined basin. Cut a piece of bread to put in the basin at this point.

Add the rest of the fruit. Cover the top of the basin with one or two slices of bread and trim the side pieces.

Spoon enough of the juice over to cover the pudding and soak in down the sides. Keep back a little of the juice.

Put a plate over the pudding and press it down, keeping the plate secured with a weight. Some juice may run out of the pudding. A plate should be slipped underneath the bowl to catch this.

When the pudding is cold, put it in the refrigerator for at least 12 hours.

When ready to serve, bring the pudding to room temperature, turn it out on to a dish and add the extra juice to any unsoaked bread.

Serve with sugar and plenty of pouring cream.

August

1 August

This August, like all Augusts, is different from other months, first because Mervyn and Maureen, our rocks, both have their annual holidays, and second because the house and garden are full of the family. This is lovely and as it should be. It means, though, that the garden, weeds included, is able to grow as it likes. We shall have time to water the greenhouse tomatoes only in the early morning, the outdoor crops in the evening and to do sporadic deadheading. Ever-optimistic Mervyn says not to worry. Yes, he does know that we have a group called Circle of Friends to see the garden on 28 August. He is sure that a week will give us plenty of time to make everything spick and span for them, but I cannot help feeling fainthearted.

2 August

We have a visit from a tree-surgeon come to straighten out a problem. Last week we found two young men from the Electricity Supply Board coolly amputating branches from trees around the back path, thinking that they were on County Council property. Their objective? To prevent interference to the high tension cables strung from the pylon in Mr McGee's field which borders the western side of the garden. This enormous pylon is a hate object for us, put there, of course, very much against our will; if any visitors look upward as they enter the garden, the pylon two hundred yards away is the first thing they see. Its great height makes it loom threateningly over the boundary trees. These intruders, by their branch cutting, have made the pylon even more visible than before.

The tree-surgeon will plant four or five fast-growing trees to fill the gap. Eucalyptus is talked of: it grows six feet a year at least. But eucalyptus is brittle, and in one of our devastating winter gales, might fall over the pylon and plunge County Wicklow into darkness. What then?

3 August

Light rain all day, endless gloom, horrible for many disappointed people on holiday especially since the weather forecasts predicted several days of brilliant sunshine. It is difficult for an enthusiastic gardener, though, not to gloat selfishly at the thought of so many roots finding refreshment. Some of our most handsome perennial plants look wilted because we skimped their mulching. Now they'll revive. As for the vegetables, this incessant rain should save the crops.

An article in today's *Irish Times* argues passionately that pesticides used in marketed vegetables and fruit account for the rapid spread of cancer. I only half believe this, but cannot help being pleased when we become nearly self-sufficient. We do use slug-killers, but they never touch the crops: otherwise pesticides are never used in the kitchen garden. We must not be self-righteous about this. It would be most difficult to grow those susceptible plants, cabbages, without using pesticides. But as our soil is so thin we just grow mainly beans, spinach and beetroot, all of them unlikely to be attacked by insects or grubs.

5 August

The rain started on Saturday, and now days later it is still raining; a trough of low pressure moved this way apparently. Weeds have doubled their size, roses hang down in sodden clusters and inside the greenhouse tomatoes and grapes drip with condensation. We are not especially unlucky: there are floods all over south-west Ireland and in France. In Eastern Europe the Oder has burst its banks, making thousands homeless. Blue skies belong to another planet: we cannot believe in them.

6 August

It is finer today. We pick all the sweet peas that are not sodden, divide them into colours, white flowers in one glass jar, mauve and purple in another and flame-coloured in a third and place them in separate rooms to give scent. No arrangement is needed for these treasures of July and August.

7 August

Humphrey, our rumbustious seven-year-old grandson, has a friend here to spend the afternoon. They are in the garden the whole time, first playing with Cora, who becomes wildly excited, and then with a frog they find in one of the lily ponds. They keep putting the frog in a small pail of water to make it give astonishing leaps. Eventually they are persuaded to put it back in the water where it hides under the prolific Canadian pondweed, which has grown like a submerged forest this summer.

There should be children here more often: the garden, with its many secret places, is fun for them. There are creatures galore around and in the ponds—ramshorn snails, and newts, waterbeetles usually in the water, coloured dragonflies and plain pondskaters flitting over the surface. It is the ponds, though, that make the garden dangerous for toddlers, who always have to be supervised when playing there.

8 August

The sun comes out at last and the world lights up. We spread a hay mulch over the roots of the runner beans to preserve their moisture because suddenly the day is very hot indeed. The dahlia-type bulbs we planted to make a purple group in the gravel garden have turned out to have orange flowers. I throw them, crossly, on the eternal flame, and hurry to the nursery to replace them with crimson verbena. These should be in full flower by the time our visitors come. Instant gardening!

9 August

The heat goes on. We look exhausted and so does the garden. People are booking tickets to go to the north of Scotland and even to the Arctic Circle just to get cool. What do they do there? Our star border plant this month, the purple-flowered thalictrum, is falling about with tiredness. We must keep it alive, it is so elegant. The soft fruit and vegetables are now in much better shape than the flowers. We have just enjoyed our last summer pudding of the season, full of red and black currants and a few lingering raspberries.

13 August

Gardeners are impossible people: we live too much in the future and are boringly dissatisfied with 'now'. In winter we long for spring flowers; in spring, plagued by dandelions and by rough winds, we wish it were high summer. There is a brief moment at midsummer when the controlled abundance seems perfect, but summer flowers are short-lived. By August we find an array of bedraggled plants and long for September's bracing days, when flowers last longer, weeds grow more slowly and the kitchen garden comes into its own.

15 August

I look critically at the double border, thinking about what our group will see in a fortnight. The scabious and the purple-flowered thalictrum are falling all over the place and must be propped up for the third time: this and trimming should keep them in flower. The Japanese anemones will start blooming next week: we have large groups of pink, white and dark rose ones. The two

plumed hydrangea have creamy flowers and they, making a loose frame on each side of John's new steps up to the wood, will form the most magical view in the garden.

It is good that the gravel garden borders are well equipped for late summer, with groups of silver-leaved and blue-flowered plants, relieved by dashes of crimson. All of them are sun lovers and seem happy in their placing.

18 August

Friends this evening are talking of Glanleam Garden on Valentia Island, origin of the 'Glanleam Gold' myrtle. The garden is neglected: nature has taken over, ruthlessly helped by the damp Kerry climate. So sad!

20 August

Two catastrophes.

The abutilon by the gravel garden, with its hundreds of pale blue flower-clusters every May, is suddenly half-dead. Mervyn, back from his holiday, is cutting off the withered half and we pray for the rest to hold its own. And now he tells me that the kitchen garden potatoes have blight, that ghastly consequence of a wet Irish June. He is stolid as always, but I am alarmed. We shall burn all the hulks, and spray the remaining potatoes, luckily growing on a sunny bank, and hope that their position will save them. This is the first potato blight we have suffered in thirty years at Knockmore. All other vegetables are flourishing at last, black beans and yellow courgettes looking as interesting as we had hoped: the reddish lettuce is frilly as it should be.

22 August

Why is a beautiful morning so much more marvellous than a fine afternoon? Perhaps because of the freshness and because it makes the garden a paradise for suddenly released creatures. There has been gentle rain all night but soon after dawn the sun shines, bringing out happy bees and butterflies.

John picks a basket of marrows, now doubling their size in half a day. We shall eat stuffed marrow this evening and will prepare the rest for marrow, ginger and whiskey jam, to be made tomorrow; we enjoy it for breakfast.

23 August

Another disastrous day! The marrow jam takes a long three hours to make and then fills only four small jars. The hours are not so precious, though, because it rains all day until six p.m. Let's face it: we are not going to catch up with the weeding by the 28th, not at all. The Circle of Friends (the organiser sounds so pleasant on the telephone) may wish that they had never thought of coming to Knockmore.

Cora has disappeared after most helpfully chasing a rabbit out of the kitchen garden. She cannot be found and after much calling we abandon her for the night.

24 August

John finds Cora, stuck in undergrowth after a wet night outside. She is soaking, hungry and subdued, but otherwise in fair shape. Her collar had been caught on a tree root.

26 August

Time before our group arrives seems more precious every minute. I spend a happy two hours pruning and tidying the raspberry canes for next year: this gives me a satisfying feeling of good husbandry. But the red currant bushes, we are appalled to notice, are covered with a bright green curtain of bindweed, one of our three deadly enemies! The other two are ground elder and winter heliotrope. In many ways the tale of Knockmore garden is the hand to hand battle with these three horrors. We grub up the bindweed, but only superficially.

27 August

A fierce gale last night blew over our wigwam of sweet pea and the climbing rose 'Kew Rambler' with its support. Because of the blustery weather, we decide to concentrate on consoling tomorrow's visitors with an extra warm welcome, plenty of strong coffee and home-made biscuits. Then they can be taken out into the wet, exhausted-looking garden. I make dozens of biscuits for them, sweet, little and well spiced with cinnamon.

We don't usually provide refreshments, we are simply too few to take on this extra task, and besides there are plenty of excellent tea-rooms in Enniskerry, half a mile away. But this is an exception.

28 August

We need not have worried. The Circle of Friends are very happy with everything. Rebecca, our granddaughter, and Maureen ply them with steaming coffee and plenty of biscuits. Meanwhile the sun starts to shine outside. John gives a talk about Knockmore: Mervyn answers questions. The garden does not let us down. The flowers bloom abundantly, the crops look appetising and the wood is a haven of tranquillity.

30 August

We have the usual flat feeling after an enjoyable group visit. As well as that I am nagged by the menace of time passing, a terror that strikes to the heart of many gardeners. The neglect of Glanleam Garden started this train of thought, and then at the other extreme, the obliteration of my mother's garden by new buildings. Will this garden survive? Life here is absorbing: it is also exhausting and expensive. But if we go what will it mean? A thousand spring bulbs in the wild garden murdered to make a swimming pool? Our fertile kitchen garden, manured for a hundred years, flattened for a barren tennis court? People like to have these things, why shouldn't they? But never in this garden, I hope.

Recipe for August:
Stuffed Marrow

We make this savoury dish several times in the late summer. Cottage cheese mixed with herbs can be substituted for the tomato.

INGREDIENTS
Serves four.

1 medium-sized marrow
4 tomatoes
500 g/1 lb fresh lamb mince
sprig of thyme
sprig of marjoram
salt
freshly ground black pepper

METHOD
Peel the marrow and scrape out the seeds. Divide it into four or eight pieces. Boil these until they are tender but still firm. Arrange the pieces in a baking dish.

Blanch the tomatoes by putting them in boiling water for about a minute, then into cold water. The skins should then peel off easily.

Mash the tomatoes and spread the mash in the hollows of the marrow pieces.

Mix the mince with the herbs, salt and pepper. Form into balls and heap onto the tomato. The tomato makes a refreshing layer between the mince and the marrow.

Bake for 25 minutes, or until the mince is a rich brown, with the oven at gas mark 5/190°C/375°F.

Serve this succulent marrow without potatoes but with fresh runner beans.

September

The front of the house

1 September

The year's cycle makes a rapid shift in September. Have the stifling days and the constant interruptions of summer finished? Today is refreshingly cool, a bright, windless day. Hidden birds sing as though it were spring, while butterflies and bees suck nectar from the buddleia and hebe flowers. We harvest vegetables strenuously. The fennel is thin but eatable.

Stupidly we expect all deciduous leaves to change colour in September, but only the leaves on our prominent horse chestnut tree do. They are already showing the terracotta colours that will redden so vividly during the month. The well-grown tree, so easily seen from our front windows, signals the changing seasons; it is the very first tree to colour in autumn, and in spring its leaf buds are the earliest of all to open, giving us the fresh green we long for.

4 September

I walk up and down the double border this morning worrying about the Japanese anemones, some of our favourite plants. We have pink, white and dark red ones. Yesterday evening I opened Nancy Mitford's *The Pursuit of Love* at the page where she trounces the gardens of Surrey for their 'huge and hideous flowers . . . if possible of a different colour from what nature intended.' She singled out dark brown irises. I see her point. So are our 'Prinz Friedrich' anemones, such a rich dark rose colour, too different from the normal pink or white? What had someone done to make them that colour? They have double flowers too, a bad sign; pink and white anemones are always single. And Rosemary, who knows best, told us firmly that she liked the white ones better. But there's no going back. We love all our Japanese anemones and the groups of 'Prinz Friedrich', blooming near sky-blue scabious and purple thalictrum, give a special warmth to the autumn borders.

7 September

I picked, peeled and chopped a large marrow last night, mixed it with sliced lemon, showered it with sugar and a little water and left it to soak. This morning I make marrow jam. The added whiskey bubbles frighteningly when poured in but eventually settles down. The golden jam smells so delicious that we are sure to finish it in a week.

9 September

More jam. This time with fruit from a Victoria plum tree. The jam is well set and a soft red colour. I cook plums in red wine as a simple pudding.

10 September

Great excitement: Enniskerry has a good report from the Tidy Towns inspectors; it is one of the best-kept villages in County Wicklow. Mervyn and others have worked hard in their spare time to improve the two little streets, now a picture of fresh paint, pretty shop signs, hanging baskets and window-boxes. All this overlays attractive estate village architecture, with a central clocktower as a focal point. Well-tended roses have brightened the village throughout the summer months.

12 September

Most of this garden is on the south side of the house, hidden from approaching eyes. Our avenue is on the east side and runs through shaggy fields. The narrow borders at the front of the house are tortured by the east wind, so are sparsely stocked with hydrangeas and hellebores. A few years ago we decided to give visitors a foretaste of flowers on their arrival by collecting all our autumn cyclamen plants and spreading them under two trees—the pine at the top of the avenue and the deodar cedar at the other side of the house; from this cedar you can see the flower garden floating below.

The change has worked well: given tree roots, which

they need and love, autumn cyclamen require no attention except weeding. The flowers make a tentative approach in late July; they are in full bloom by the end of August. Just now leaves are joining the little flowers and the two colonies are spread out like tapestries. By mid-November the flowers will have disappeared but the pretty ivy-shaped leaves will stay until May.

13 September

Susan, who has come from Somerset for her annual visit, has chosen to sleep in the skylight room, where she has no view, but likes to see leaves moving against a blue sky. Our other guest room has a window far too wide for its size, giving a panorama of the garden and the mountain but killing all cosiness. Susan, a friend from university days, has been coming to stay for thirty years, at first shaking her head over our lunacy in taking on this garden, but very gradually coming round. Now she loves the place and likes our latest improvements, the steps to the wood and the small bridge.

Susan herself has a small, brilliantly coloured garden round a fast-flowing stream; people come to admire it from far away. Her rocky slopes make formality impossible—luckily, because she intensely dislikes gardens with straight lines and clipped shrubs. With the zeal of an evangelist, I take her to Killruddery this afternoon to see its great formal garden.

Many people would call Killruddery garden a park. It was created in the late seventeenth century in the

The rosebeds

grand manner for the fourth Earl of Meath, whose descendants still live there. The layout is believed to have been designed by a pupil of André Le Nôtre, creator of Louis XIV's garden at Versailles; Killruddery is one of the very few Irish or British gardens designed in the classic French tradition, with long canals, *allées*, basins and a lime avenue extending over the skyline. Visitors are impressed when told of the garden's antiquity. Killruddery's dignified beauty is equally lovely winter and summer.

We enjoy a peaceful walk beside the canals and a visit to the sylvan theatre, thought to have been dug out and hedged in the eighteenth century. We wonder if there is another garden theatre in these islands dating from so long ago. We ramble through the Victorian section of lavender, box and pink roses and admire the ornamental dairy. Is Susan converted to the occasional straight line? I hope so.

15 September

We come back from a visit to the nursery with eight dozen blue-flowered *Anemone blanda*, bulbs to plant in full sun in front of the little cottage. They bloom much too early in the year to be seen by visiting groups, but their flowers will lure us out into the fresh air on fine February mornings. Susan and I look closely at the weeds in the gravel garden and find that many of them are not weeds at all but the glossy, heart-shaped leaves of *Cyclamen coum*, the cyclamen that comes into bloom before the snowdrops, and lasts until they have withered. This cyclamen is hard to control: it jumps from where we plant it to where it wants to grow, which seems now to be in the middle of our gravel. For once nature, instead of being perverse, preventing germination, killing young plants and creating a hundred other horrors, has helped the garden by blowing cyclamen seeds to where both flowers and leaves will look their best, set off by clean gravel. No weedkiller after all, just tender loving care.

17 September

The tree-surgeon is back again today about suitable trees to hide the grotesque Electricity Supply Board pylon. As tall-growing trees as possible, we thought eucalyptus, aspen, red oak. We do not make a final choice but, over tea, he gives us a talk about planting any tree. There are cheap holes and expensive holes, he says, and holes are the key to successful tree-growing. Cheap holes are small and unmanured. The trees are given no aftercare: weeds and grass are allowed to surge round the trunks, preventing rain from reaching the roots. The trees will be puny and will probably die. Expensive holes are made expensive by labour. Holes are large, well-watered and manured. Weeds and grass are kept well away from the trunks for many years. Watering is not forgotten, especially during a dry May. Such trees should live and flourish.

Something clicks. Years ago I saw a tree in a local estate that had been planted by a VIP. But it was a cheap hole tree, had been completely neglected and was withering away.

21 September

This morning, between mouthfuls of toast and marmalade, John asks what those things outside the front door are? Had some crates of wine arrived after dark, I wondered? No, it is those plants, our forty-year-old hydrangeas! It is extraordinary that John, so sensitive

about the trees in his wood, so clever about their grouping and care, should hardly know the names of any flowers. The hydrangeas he speaks of are especially opulent just now and the flowers a subtle greenish white with pink tones. From the side, our pillared house looks more romantic than usual, emerging from their blowsy overblown blooms.

22 September

A lot of noise at eight-thirty this morning when Jimmy McCabe and his merry men arrive with a truck, a powerful digger and some bright yellow flexible pipes, like convulsive pythons. At the moment Mr McGee's field spills all its surplus water into the top of our garden, with dire results to our cherished stone terraces. The men are to make a third attempt to prevent the terraces from collapsing; yet again they are showing ominous cracks after bouts of torrential rain.

Unfortunately the designer of our drainage operation is out of action; he fell off a ladder yesterday while picking his apple crop. John is having to help direct the water channels and is enjoying this very much.

23 September

Apple-picking time. Mervyn is scything round the large apple tree this morning and for the first time for many years rootles round behind it: 'that tree at the back, the small one, has nice-looking apples on it.' A faint chord strikes in my mind and after making my way through

agonising nettles, I find a small, misshapen 'Cox's Orange Pippin' tree. It had been planted twenty-five or so
years ago and had been forgotten for at least fifteen,
devoured by the great Bramley and by rampant weeds,
but struggling to live and, surprisingly, producing some
ruddy fruit. The little tree needs light and nurture. A
pleasant winter task will be to prune and revive the two
apple trees: the large one may need pruning by someone more expert than us.

27 September

Rosemary comes to lunch, bringing two clumps of
hesperis plants for the double border; hesperis have pretty
old-fashioned flowers in pale mauve and purple going
up to a spike. Like many traditional flowers, they have
several romantic names: sweet rocket, damask violet,
and, I find in an old book, dames' violets and queen's
gillyflowers. The book was the *Paradisi* of John
Parkinson, the king's herbarist, and was published in
1629. Parkinson gives a thorough account of the
hesperis, and shows a print of the plant too, stiff and
formal but still recognisably *Hesperis matronalis*. He
explains its mysterious name: it is Greek for 'of an
evening' and was given to the plant because the flowers
smell especially sweet at dusk. Hesperis, I remember,
was a name for the evening star.

Parkinson's account of the hesperis is so interesting
that I am encouraged to read his views on peach-leaved
campanulas; we have been frustrated about ours for sev-

eral years, finding that the ones carefully planted to stream through the double border fade in too short a time. This year we notice that the few growing in shady places are larger and longer-lived than the others. I have never seen this commented on until finding it mentioned in the *Paradisi*:

> the root is very small white and threddy, creeping under the upper crust of the ground, so that often times the heat and drought of summer will go near to parch and wither it utterly; it requireth therefore to be planted in some shadowie place.

Thank you, John Parkinson, apothecary of London, for your garden advice from nearly four hundred years ago. We have already discussed transplanting some of these campanula into shadier ground. We shall hesitate no longer.

Recipe for September: Plums in Red Wine

There is often a glut of Victoria plums in September.

INGREDIENTS

Serves four.

750 g/1½ lbs Victoria plums

90 g/3 oz sugar

120 ml/4 fl oz water

juice of one orange

250 ml/½ pint red wine

METHOD

Rinse the plums. Split them open along their grooves, twist the halves and prise out the stones.

Bring the water and orange juice to the boil in a saucepan. Put in the sugar and simmer for a few minutes until it is dissolved.

Add the wine and simmer for another minute. Put in the plum halves, cover the saucepan and move it off the stove. Let the plums just steep in the syrup for 10 or 15 minutes. They will keep their shape.

Take out the plums with a slotted spoon and transfer them to a warm serving dish.

Boil the syrup fast to reduce and thicken it. When it is reduced by one-third pour it over the warm plum halves.

Serve them warm with sugar and pouring cream. These plums can be served cold and will taste stronger.

If you are feeding children, you probably should not use wine but water; the plums will still taste good. The wine, though, is healthy for adults and for the elderly.

October

3 October

There are split hazelnut shells on the woodland paths, the sign of red squirrels at work, gnawing holes in the tops of the shells, splitting them skilfully in two and removing the nuts. Then this evening Mervyn sees a squirrel under the big Spanish chestnut tree, rooting around for chestnuts blown down by last night's storm. There should be squirrels' nests in our wood, large nests, twiggy and well fitted into a tree fork. We have searched for them dozens of times, but so far have not found a single one.

Wild life is coming nearer. Last night John saw a badger sauntering across the road into our cowslip field. We abhor badgers. They throw up earth in the wrong places and can devour hundreds of useful worms in one night. We hope that Cora, running about outside all day, and Alexander, our old cat, prowling all night, will keep badgers from the garden as efficiently as they keep away rabbits and rats.

No one remembers how old Alexander is. Years ago we were given, we thought, a handsome, tortoiseshell tom kitten and called it Alexander. After three carefree months the kitten suddenly became pear-shaped and gave birth to three kittens of her own, all in about twelve hours. She was an appalling mother: her kittens had to be fed with a pipette while Alexander eloped with a black tom cat. John eventually caught Alexander, locking her in a shed with her kittens until they were reared: then she was firmly neutered. She spends the nights outside chasing wild creatures and the days lying on a chair or a bed indoors.

5 October

Sad to see all our pretty colchicum flattened after a night of heavy rain. The genuine autumn crocuses, *Crocus speciosus*, more fragile to look at than the colchicum, are standing up well. I look up colchicum in an old encyclopaedia and find that they should never be in a bare bed, which is exactly where ours are. As soon as they stop flowering, they must be moved to nooks and crannies in the rockery.

6 October

Spend a strenuous afternoon with Mervyn pruning 'Kew Rambler' and 'Sanders' White', both such prolific rambler roses. We cut down all the old flowering shoots and tie up the fresh ones. Our hands are torn to pieces and our clothes too. My gardening gloves are a write-off, but it is an hour or two well spent if the roses perform as we wish by next July. They will look from many angles like fountains of blossom.

7 October

Sheila comes for her last two-hour stint in the border this year. We shall miss her cheerful face and cherry-coloured trousers every Tuesday morning. She and I drink strong coffee on the veranda and discuss dahlias. Fashions in gardening have changed again. Some years ago dahlias, props of every autumn garden, were pronounced to be too gaudy. For a long time few élite gardeners grew them. Now the reaction has set in. Pastel colours, so pretty and prevalent, have been declared anaemic, needing badly to be rescued by groups of dahlias like 'Arabian Night', deep red, or 'Bishop of Llandaff', scarlet.

Sheila and I, who have similar tastes in plants, decide to enliven the silver and blue borders round the gravel garden next year, not with dahlias—difficult plants to rear anyway—but with groups of dark rose cosmos; they are tall, more delicate-looking than dahlias, and are easy to grow from seed.

10 October

The dark side of autumn today: sleet instead of rain, rough winds, neither planting nor blackberry-picking weather. Leaves are blocking all the outside drains. We dare not light the winter room fire because I have not been able to find the sweep. All is bleak. Why do we struggle on? Why not live in the South of France where the temperature is 20° Celsius now and where we find it so lovely every March. The answer: because apart from the pain of leaving one's own country, we would hate the scorching summers, the dusty palm trees, the crowds, the swimming pool life. Our garden and its temperamental four seasons keep us nourished, physically with fresh air and exercise, and mentally by forcing us to plan projects for the year ahead.

12 October

Bombarded by marrows! We eat them most days as a vegetable; we stuff them with delicious mince; we make them, laboriously, into jam; we give them away. We are always thrilled when the season starts, but now we shall go insane if the marrows last another week.

13 October

Our vegetables have done well this year after a slow, cold start. Our yellow tomatoes were exceptionally sweet: they looked pretty sliced and arranged with red ones.

14 October

I am preparing breakfast when the telephone rings. It is a girl from Bord Fáilte (the tourist board), who reads out a glowing description of our garden for their brochure. It does not include the kitchen garden, which many people enjoy: they like a bit of down-to-earthery. So we squeeze the kitchen garden into the notice. The board has added 'French spoken' to its description, rather a worry. I have looked up herbaceous border, deciduous, biennial, pollinators and so on in a French dictionary dozens of times and still cannot remember the right words. They will have to be written on a card and glanced at surreptitiously.

16 October

A fine morning. I go into the fields to pick blackberries but am nearly driven back by surging, mooing cattle. There is not a blade of grass in the front fields, so I shoo the hungry animals into the cowslip field, still green. I make blackberry and apple jam this evening.

20 October

Another beautiful morning, calm and bright. The three kinds of Japanese anemones, pink, white and dark rose, are blooming happily. The jasmine nightshade, falling in a white cascade above the gravel garden, has more flowers than ever before. Butterflies and winged insects are making last efforts to suck nectar from cerotostigma blooms. But last night was cold. I feel like the mother of fine sons when a world war is coming, savouring the precious

The south side of the house

moments but threatened by an ominous future.

24 October

I take a bunch of our 'Muscat of Alexandria' grapes to a ninety-four-year-old friend, a great gardener who not long ago grew three flourishing 'Black Hamburg' grapevines, two peach trees and one apricot tree in her long lean-to greenhouse. She was always generous with her carefully tended fruit; no summer passed without her many friends enjoying her juicy white peaches and succulent grapes.

Thinking about her makes me notice how very long many gardeners live, some of them famous, but many more known only to their friends and families. We ourselves have known several who stayed active into their nineties. I spend the evening scrutinising books on garden history and quickly find no fewer than fifty-two celebrated gardener botanists who lived well beyond their eightieth year. Thirty of these belonged to or overlapped with the Victorian age, but the remainder were alive in the seventeenth and eighteenth centuries when the expectation of life was just thirty years. I am pleased to find a few well-known people born or resident in Ireland among these veterans.

First Sir Hans Sloane, the distinguished founder of the Chelsea Physic Garden, who lived into his nineties. After being brought up at Killyleagh, County Down, he spent little time in Ireland. The next in chronological order is Mrs Delany (1700–88), a friend of Swift and mistress of Delville, a delightful small estate in north County Dublin. Although she had no formal training (no woman did), she was absorbed in botany and gardening, and at the age of seventy-two made botanically correct cut-out pictures of plants, both attractive and useful for identification. They are admired and exhibited today.

We must not forget the greatest Irish horticulturist of them all: William Robinson (1838–1935), who with book after book and incessant magazine articles created interest in natural gardening for an enormous public. The most generous to Ireland of our long-lived gardener-botanists were Sir Frederick and Lady Moore. Sir Frederick was curator of the National Botanic Garden. This robust pair, both of them living until their nineties, were famous for their kindness with and advice about interesting plants.

A fascinating gardener-botanist who worked mainly outside Ireland was Charlotte Cuffe of Leyrath, County Kilkenny. Married to an engineer working in Burma, she became enthralled by the flora of that country and discovered two unknown rhododendrons in the wild. During her long stay in Burma, she created an interesting botanic garden at Maymyo, not far from Mandalay. Happily, this important garden, now tended by the state, survives in spite of Burma's cruel politics: Lady Cuffe died at Leyrath in 1965, aged ninety-nine.

Why did all these people live so long? Genes? Fresh air and exercise? These must have helped, but I suspect that a secret was zest, fired by curiosity. They experimented with plants and looked forward to the future with avid interest. Would their patient plans succeed? The anticipation kept them alert, happy and in good health.

26 October

I am checking on our trees' autumn colouring this morning. No one could say that all leaves have changed colour. The oaks and ashes are still a strong green. The maples, lime tree, Spanish chestnut, sycamore and beeches look only dusted with red or yellow, but all the birch leaves are pale yellow, the leaves on the handsome snowdrop tree are pale gold, and as for the giant cherry, when the sun shines on its shimmering red and gold leaves, we forget that autumn is such a long, slow agony.

28 October

We must not mope about the sadness of autumn. It is a new beginning. Now we can move plants safely, shape bushes, reconstruct garden features. Mervyn is already preparing for next year by spreading leaf-mould over well-weeded beds in the kitchen garden, to help fertilise the soil. I go to the nursery for a *Viburnum* X *burkwoodii*, such a pretty shiny-leaved plant, to extend a shrub border. While there, I ask about cheap tunnel cloches to warm up the kitchen garden soil before the spring sowing; this spring our seeds all died of cold. Other people said the same, but I noticed that Rosemary was successful with her seeds. Next year I hope we shall be as I bought some cloches.

30 October

We pick the last few bunches of grapes, a good crop this year since they had all the attention they demanded: they were carefully pruned, thinned and disciplined throughout the summer and their ventilation was not neglected.

Mervyn, well supplied with fruit trays from supermarket and grocer, is picking, sorting and storing apples. The crop from our old Bramley tree should last through the winter. He climbs his way up the large tree, filling fruit boxes and baskets and finally his anorak and its pockets. Then he comes carefully down. John is never bored with meals of cooking apples and would like to eat them every evening until the forced rhubarb is ready in March.

Recipe for October:
Blackberry and Apple Jam

The tradition is to use blackberries before Hallowe'en while they are not yet watery. Our field hedge had hundreds this year. We mixed them with a few windfall apples to make a jam in which blackberry dominates.

INGREDIENTS

Makes 2.5 kg/6 lbs of jam

1 kg/2 lbs blackberries

360 g/¾ lb cooking apples peeled, cored and chopped

159 ml/¼ pint water

juice of 1 lemon

1.5 kg/3 lbs sugar

METHOD

Simmer the blackberries in half the water and the apples in the other half. Mash them both into a pulp.

Mix the combined pulp in a large saucepan or preserving pan.

Add the lemon juice, then the sugar and stir until it is dissolved.

Boil quickly until the jam sets. Test it every few minutes by putting a dessert spoonful on a cold plate.

Wait for a minute and then push the jam with a finger. If it wrinkles, it has set.

Pour it carefully into clean warm jars, label, cover and keep in a cool dry place.

November

1 November

When we eat in the kitchen, and this is almost always, John sits facing the window. So it is that this morning at breakfast he is the first to see a red squirrel grubbing about the gravel for Spanish chestnuts. There are several little tits too, pecking at seeds and enjoying the sun. As usual, after a few minutes, two magpies break up this happy scene; the squirrel scampers up the chestnut tree and the tits dive into the bushes.

It is a beautiful morning. Halcyon, I call it, but John says No, 'halcyon' means calm at sea in midwinter. The garden does seem like a calm sea between storms though; the weather was rough yesterday and probably will be tomorrow. We can see wraith-like mists rising from the cool grass and evaporating in the sun. Nothing else moves. The cat basks her old bones against a warm south wall. By two o'clock, evening in Ireland, the sky has clouded over and the idyllic hours have passed.

5 November

I take a box full of Japanese anemone plants, white-flowered ones, to Rosemary: they are tricky to establish but will be helped by this week's wet weather. The hesperis she gave us looks alive and well in the double border.

6 November

We see the squirrel again this morning, hopping around on the grass and breaking open the chestnut husks. This time it is there for at least fifteen minutes, a long time for such a shy creature to stay in one vulnerable place. The squirrel's appetite for Spanish chestnuts makes me wonder why more of these beautiful trees are not planted. They are tall and strong, the bark is attractively spiral and the shining green leaves hang down in clusters: just now each cluster seems to have one yellow, one copper and seven vivid green leaves. The effect is brilliant. The chestnuts here never mature enough for human con-

sumption; we are happy to leave them to the squirrels,
hoping that these pretty little creatures will not strip
the bark. Grey squirrels are known to do this, but red
ones like ours are less destructive.

10 November

A letter comes this morning from a Mrs Alicia Russell,
great-niece of Charlotte and Stella May; she thanks us
for looking after the aunts' garden. A friend or relation
has sent her a glowing tribute to Knockmore garden
published in *The Irish Times*. It is a lively letter, nostalgic about happy holidays here in the troubled 1920s.
She adored the place and mentions a secret garden we
cannot identify. Mrs Russell remembers her child's eye
view of the pony and trap, used for all excursions. For
the sake of the pony, the children had to walk most of
the time round hilly Enniskerry, up hills first so that

the load would not be too heavy, but then, to their dismay, down hills, too, to save the pony's shoulders.

For the only time in any of the family's memories politics intruded:

> The IRA came to the house. . . . Aunt Charlotte had to take my mother's younger sister to the Dublin dentist. And they'd blown up the Dargle Bridge in the night. So tiresome but they got there on time. Yes there was a bit of shooting, but one paid no attention because of getting to the dentist.

Well done Charlotte May! How many of us would drive a pony through bullets to relieve a niece's toothache?

12 November

We have six beautiful magnolia trees, each of a different species. Of these, far the most magnificent is the *Magnolia denudata*: As I wrote earlier, it produces hundreds of large waxy-white flowers every March on its well-shaped leafless branches, but it has two shattering faults. The first is its position, in the middle of the summer garden where for nine months of the year its vast bulk ruins views of the borders from every direction. The second fault is also due to the tree's placing, the very centre of our worst frost pocket: this means that as we know in any March every single bloom can go jet black overnight, a dreadful sight. This magnolia may well become as huge as the horse chestnut trees in the

Phoenix Park. It is far too large to transplant, but could easily be cut down. Everyone here was horrified at the suggestion at first, but must be getting used to the idea, because this afternoon I overhear John and Mervyn discussing ways of cutting the roots.

15 November

It is ridiculous, really—we are making more work for ourselves. We are extending an awkward looking half-moon-shaped bed into a shrub border: this should lead the eye along to the white tree, as we call the *Cornus controversa* (or variegated dogwood) we planted as a focal point. Annoyingly, we are not sure how to plant a shrub border. Should the shrubs be planted with nurse plants to bring them on, the nurse plants to be taken out as soon as the shrubs grow well? Should the shrubs be underplanted with ground cover like heuchera? Every square inch of that prepared earth has to have attention. And then who will look after the new border? We shall have to find a second Sheila. Very soon we shall be roping in an army to look after this complicated garden, but if the shrub border is eventually a success, it will make a well furnished part of the summer garden.

19 November

Rain and wind are in violent partnership bringing leaves down and breaking tree branches. Channels of water are everywhere, so we fear for our cherished terraces, since the elaborate pipe system we put in to divert the water is not working. The storm has stripped off the leaves from the Spanish chestnut tree, which now looks like a great grey skeleton. However, this does make the kitchen brighter. Our road is flooded and there has been a landslide a few hundred yards below us on the Lower Dargle Road. The Dargle river is in spate and yesterday burst its banks at Tinnehinch where our ninety-four-year old neighbour lives: some years ago there was great excitement because she had to be rescued from flood water by tractor.

25 November

More torrential rains both yesterday and today. In the pitch black evening I run my car into an unexpected road lake, and have to be rescued by John and Mervyn. Luckily our old rope is strong enough to tow the car up the steep hill. We bless the cobbled drains at the side of our avenue: they take streams of running water whenever there is a rainstorm, and must have been first made over a hundred years ago to deal with the water on that slope.

26 November

We receive an interesting book by this morning's post. It is the autobiography of a naval architect, George O'Brien Kennedy, who was brought up at Knockranny, two miles from here. He knew the hospitable Miss Mays in his youth and describes them in the book as 'living in style with a smart pony and trap, a man in livery to drive them and a gardener likewise'. Mr Kennedy writes of parties Charlotte and Stella May gave for their young relations, organising parlour games and drama in the winter, and paper-chases in the summer. He fell in love with Peggy Acton, a young member of the family and then, sadly, lost all trace of her. But first love never quite goes away, he found. A few years ago Brien, as he called himself, came to this house, asking us of Peggy's whereabouts. It took time for us to trace even remote contacts: he followed up the ones we gave him, only to find that Peggy had died a few years before. This story does not betray any confidences; it is written for everyone to read in *Not all at Sea* published in 1997.

28 November

It is still pouring and has been for over a week. The only gardening that we can do is to check that the open drains are working; this we do after breakfast and again in the mid-afternoon, just before dark. This is quite enough outside activity for a miserable wet day. We do worry, though. We worry about the terraces. Will they collapse after the week's rain? John, a pessimist, can see at least two sinister bulges. Mervyn, the optimist, thinks 'everything's OK' as usual. I am cautious.

29 November

The rain has stopped at last. Early this morning we hear Cora barking shrilly and see that she is tormenting a hedgehog; she has a recognisable hedgehog bark. The little hedgehog is curled up into the tightest ball imaginable and is being bounced around by the dog. I rush

The veranda from the summer garden

outside in a flimsy dressing gown and beat Cora off:
then John takes the hedgehog a couple of hundred yards
off to a quiet part of the wood, hiding it under leaves.
Has the little arrival caught cold? It must be well into
hedgehogs' hibernation season, an uneasy thought.

Later this morning there is time to look at the garden, drab and limp after all the rain. But I find enough
winter jasmine for a small jug and some irises too. It is
noticeable that few people have time to make elaborate
flower arrangements these days; they may even be go-

ing out of fashion except for state occasions and flower festivals. I am not sorry. Arrangements had become sickeningly competitive; the flowers themselves looking most uncomfortable and sometimes with hardly any water, all to make the 'arrangement'. In the last few years it has been a pleasure to see flowers put comfortably in simple jugs round stylish rooms, with the stems given as much water as they could desire.

30 November

November seems to be the month for letters. This morning we hear from Sandy Dunbar in Scotland. He encloses the promised extracts from Phoebe Whitworth's memoirs. At first glance they look fascinating. She writes like an angel, even though, or perhaps because, she spent all her childhood abroad with her parents and only went to school for a dreadful few months. Phoebe revelled in their life in Hong Kong and Hawaii and enjoyed the family's long holidays in London and at Knockmore: it is one of these holidays that must be commemorated on our little sundial. We long to read Phoebe's memoirs, but will not have time until after Christmas.

Recipe for November: Borsch

The most warming soup imaginable. Everyone has his or her own recipe. We use beetroot from our store, or long-rooted beetroot which may be still in the ground.

INGREDIENTS

Serves four

2 large beetroot, skinned and chopped

1 leek, chopped

2 carrots, peeled and chopped

500 ml/1 pint stock or water

1 teaspoon salt

1 teaspoon sugar

thyme

3 tomatoes, skinned and chopped

4 tablespoons cream or yogurt (if liked)

METHOD

Bring the beetroot, leek and carrots to the boil in the stock. Add the salt, sugar and thyme. Simmer until the vegetables are soft.

Put everything through the liquidiser.

Reheat, add the chopped tomato and simmer for five minutes. This gives a fresh taste.

Stir in cream or yogurt and serve at once.

December

1 December

The garden is looking battered after streaming rain and violent wind. Branches and leaves litter the ground. All the trees are bare except for the oaks: their leaves are still a rich golden brown. People write lyrically about the stillness and peace of December gardens, but this one is not often still in December, and on the occasions when it is peaceful, much of it is covered with a dangerous frost.

Rosemary stands by the winter room window this morning. 'It is like a summer garden out there,' she says, and she is right. We are all looking at a corner of blue grey teucrium and purple sage. White-flowered solanum hang over these and, lower down, a little parahebe is blooming for the second time. In this sheltered sunny corner semi-tender plants will grow happily, even when the main garden is devastated.

4 December

Five friends come to lunch, all sociable so that talk flows freely. It is gratifying to be able to give them home-grown spinach and potatoes with the rack of lamb. Mervyn's optimism was justified; the main crop of potatoes escaped the dreaded blight. We all enjoy the Apple Charlotte, made from brown sugar, bread, butter and lots of our apples, a comfort food everyone calls it. The same pudding, or nearly the same, is called Brown Betty in the United States and is there made with golden syrup: it was always the favourite children's pudding in the old days.

5 December

Mervyn and I are walking past the lily ponds this morning, sighing because one is leaking and wondering whether the rampant Canadian pondweed will devour the lilies, when he forks out some green slime: clinging to it is the tiniest newt, about half an inch long. It is unmistakably a newt, bulging eyes, four short legs and a long tail. We put it straight back to wallow in the mud, hoping it will survive the winter down there if the ponds ice over, as they surely will.

This makes me think about other wild creatures. The badger John saw crossing the road has not been seen since. Our squirrel has made off with most of the sweet chestnuts and disappeared. We hope the hedgehogs have gone to ground in the wood because it is high time they hibernated. Garden birds have started to come to their food table, especially a robin, which puts off the others. Robins' cosy looks conceal aggressive instincts.

7 December

A bitterly cold dark day with sleety showers. But we have fun narrowing the old laurel arch leading to the high walk. We plant young laurels and viburnum on each side. Then we narrow the wide steps up to the arch with dwarf evergreen plants. This should concentrate the view through the arch to an inviting glimpse of the high walk; views and inviting glimpses are all important in a garden, not easy to arrange when you take over an old garden with solid immovable structures. But the view through the laurel arch does not disappoint; jasmine, planted the whole length of the sunny wall, flowers all winter and in the summer the long lavender bed takes over. Through the next arch, in the beech hedge, there is no inviting glimpse, just an old well-proportioned greenhouse, excellent for growing grapes, but imperviously blocking the view of a tree-lined path.

The wood in winter

12 December

A terrible night with rain pouring and wind howling: a huge ivy covered branch has landed on the guinea pig shed, so called because it once housed the children's guinea pig. The garden looks tired out by the 'wrackful siege of battering days'. It is time to fix the shutters at three-thirty. Gloom! No wonder everyone starts giving parties and over-eating in December to raise their spirits.

We are keeping our end up this weekend by giving two parties, each for thirty people. It is too early for a Christmas tree but we shall make a gesture towards Christmas by assembling half-porcupines of berried holly, winter jasmine and laurustinus and putting them in bowls all over the hall and drawing-room. Hydrangea, beautiful though they are, are too sombre to bring in at Christmas time.

15 December

A violent east wind today, like a blizzard without the snow. When we open the front door, the house feels ripped apart. I cower by our crackling fire in the west-facing winter room. As early as three o'clock the sky is darkening so quickly that we shutter the windows for an evening indoors.

I had made one expedition outside to see if the evergreen rose 'Adélaïde d'Orléans' had kept its leaves in the bitter weather. Yes, the leaves were still there and the plant none the worse. By coincidence, we had seen the name 'd'Orléans' this morning: it was the name of a painter Louise d'Orléans. The painting, an exquisite one of an iris, was reproduced on a card printed for the Fitzwilliam Museum in Cambridge: it gave Louise d'Orléans' dates as 1812–52, but nothing more.

Who were these women, Adélaïde d'Orléans and Louise d'Orléans? They were flower-lovers obviously. There were a few books on our shelves that might help us discover: an old encyclopaedia, *Nouveau Petit Larousse*, William Paul's *The Rose Garden* (1848), and a more recent work *Climbing Roses Old and New* by Graham Stuart Thomas. A picture emerges. Several outstanding evergreen roses were bred in the 1820s by Monsieur Jacques, head gardener to the Duc d'Orléans, at the Château de Neuilly. The best-known were 'Adélaïde d'Orléans' and 'Félicité, et Perpétué': these are still obtainable. Less well known were 'Princesse Marie' and 'Princesse Louise'.

In 1830 the Duc d'Orléans became Louis Philippe, King of the French, as he called himself. His daughter Louise became a much-loved Queen of Belgium: there was nothing in our books about her talents as a flower painter, but her dates of birth and death are the same as those on the card except for two years. There is more to find out when we have time.

Good old Larousse, terse but definite, has an entry for Adélaïde. She was Louis Philippe's sister and wise counsellor. This boring king came from, and produced, a talented family. Adélaïde died in 1847, the year before her brother was forced to abdicate: he could not govern France, the ungovernable. Adélaïde's robust rose, with its dangling clusters of flowers, is uniquely beautiful.

A corner of the summer garden

17 December

The weather is kinder today, though damp and grey everywhere. A day for Christmas cooking. But I take a few minutes outside to trim leaves of two hellebores, one with pink flowers and one with white. Both of them are obligingly flowering early for Christmas and will be admired by many because they are on either side of the front door.

On the way down to the eternal flame with the trimmings, I pass a bare branched tree, winter sweet, and had a sudden vision of it, pruned and shaped and made into an ideal host for a rambler rose. I mention this to Mervyn, always one for immediate action, and before you can say 'knife' we are down in the garden thinning the tree branches and then digging up and pruning our 'Kew Rambler'. Until now it had been inadequately supported first by a rotting apple tree and then by a feeble iron obelisk. So we plant the rose under the tree and dream of generous pink clusters of 'Kew Rambler' reaching out to the July sunshine and dominating the little rose borders. We are exhilarated to be constructive at a time of year when all seems disintegrating. Damp greyness is ignored. Christmas cooking is forgotten.

21 December

The winter solstice is today, or maybe it is tomorrow. Whichever it is, things can only get better now, or rather get brighter, oh so gradually. Usually the worst weather comes after the end of December, when we always imagine we are halfway through winter, pathetically, as winter continues until late March here.

We have finished eating our tomatoes: the crop has supplied us for nearly five months. Other home-grown vegetables still feeding us are spinach, getting old and reedy, leeks, sparsely planted, and the excellent 'Rooster' potatoes; red-skinned and smooth, they would grace the shelves of a high powered supermarket.

The red squirrel is here again this morning, as usual at breakfast time. It runs from the ground, up the weeping cherry tree, onto the Spanish chestnut, swinging from branch to branch over to the neighbouring Monterey pine until it disappears into the pine's dark depths.

23 December

The squirrel is back yet again for nuts this morning. It is making a habit of coming if the weather is mildish. Cora only finds its scent after it has scampered up the tree and she does not seem excited.

We have a reaction against Christmas trees, partly because there are no suitable trees to cut from our wood, partly from laziness and partly from the urge to be different. There are no small children coming to see us over Christmas, so why not give our tired baubles and silver bells a year's rest. We bring in from the veranda a five-foot high *Pelargonium graveolens*, (we always call it lemon-scented geranium) and place it in a corner of the front hall. The fresh green filigree leaves look pretty against our terracotta walls and the air is now full of a lemon scent. The presents will go beneath it, just as they would round a Christmas tree.

Another scent will be of oranges, orange *pot pourri*. Every evening I cut thin slices of orange and put them in the Rayburn stove's cool oven; in the morning they are dry and a rich brown colour. They are to be spread on blue willow pattern plates together with scored, dried tangerines, bay leaves and sprigs of silver-leaved plants from the garden. Strong orange essence will be sprinkled over this intriguing mixture.

24 December

A horrific day all over the country; eighty mile an hour winds, driving rain, trees and branches crashing down and electricity poles suddenly collapsing. Our opposite neighbours had a thick beech branch fall onto the unlit road, blocking all traffic. They work to remove it heroically by eleven-thirty pm with the storm raging round them all the time. No ferries sail and Cork and Kerry are plunged in darkness for the whole evening. Cork and Shannon airports are closed to traffic.

25 December

Christmas Day. The storm dies down slowly. The southwest of Ireland is without power and so without refrigerators and many stoves. All those turkeys waiting to be roasted! We just have time to look round for damage. There are plenty of branches littering the ground and one arbutus tree has fallen but has done no harm. Some irises have struggled into bud in spite of the turbulence. I pick them, to unfurl in the warm house.

27 December

At last the garden shows December's stillness. The wind has dropped, but it is the cold stillness of exhaustion, of sodden fallen leaves and branches flattened, not the stillness of serenity.

We watch a documentary about the natural world this evening. Rather horrible, We always think that our garden is a paradise of peaceful, purring, chirping and buzzing creatures. How wrong we are! The film showed that for the whole of spring and summer wild creatures are mating, eating and murdering, no less: then, in late autumn, except for the hibernators, they are dying. Our favourite red squirrels devour nestling birds, the birds devour harmless worms, pretty newts kill everything they can. Ponds are not peaceful places but are full of carnage. It made me wonder about the Garden of Eden. Were all those birds and animals vegetarian or did they just not need feeding?

31 December

New Year's Eve. Another year has passed struggling with nature at Knockmore. It was good for shrubs, roses, herbaceous plants, bad for the first vegetables because spring and early summer were dry. It was bad for visitors (or some of them) because of a record wet June. This winter so far has been, in spite of violent storms, fairly mild.

Today is the perfect winter day that we were waiting for, cold, still and bright. Irises are opening in the sun. I pick four white and six mauve ones and mix them with the inevitable winter jasmine in a china jug. Yellow, mauve and white turn out to be a mixture of great delicacy. Outside rhubarb chard, deep crimson, looks striking, hellebore flowers mellow, and box is a fresh green after the rainy season. Our white-flowered periwinkle flowers all over its sunny bank: it flowers most months of the year, we do not know why.

A long and peaceful evening. There is time to read Phoebe Whitworth's childhood memories, of coming to Knockmore before the Great War to stay with the Miss Mays.

> We spent the Easter holidays that year [1906] in Ireland with our aunts at Knockmore. . . . Knockmore garden in spring was something out of this world. We had never seen masses of bulbs coming up through the grass under fruit trees just bursting into blossom. We had never seen terraces with pergolas and Italian vases full of flowers . . . We had never seen such a garden built in the cup of the hills, with a peep through the woods of the distant sea. There were Chinese elephants . . . bearing plant pots on their heads. The roof of the veranda was decorated with green dragons which daddy had sent from Hong Kong and down at the bottom of the field in front of the house was a gypsy caravan where we often played and had tea.

A few years later Phoebe and her sister Stella came again—the visit commemorated on our sundial, we think:

> The aunts had made a spare room out of the loft over the stables and here Stella and I slept. It was reached by an outside staircase like a glorified ladder and had a long low window seat overlooking that queen of gardens. I remember the soft

Irish air blowing in at the window and puffing out the flowered curtains when we woke our first morning. The birds were singing and we would soon be having breakfast on the verandah where the Chinese elephants stood. We would have stir-about in Italian bowls and the butter and marmalade would be on little Italian dishes. Everything would be perfect . . .

A tiny fragment of civilisation died with the Miss Mays. Educated to use their leisure, they spent their talents generously to interest young people from all walks of life. Phoebe and Stella were some of the first of many children looked after by their aunts at Knockmore. They were taught how to sketch, to find wild flowers and water creatures, taken caravanning and given well-chosen books to read. Games were imaginative, charades and paper-chases. There were fancy dress parties. It is sad that today's families have little time for these simple but interesting pursuits.

As for the garden nowadays, the Mays would still know it. There have been some changes: the kitchen garden is more formal, the double border is shorter; the Chinese elephants and the green dragons are missing; the wood is happily now incorporated in the garden. The genius of the place has been preserved, the borders of campanulas and old roses, the heaving box hedges, the hundreds of naturalised spring flowers are all still there. And the garden is still a romantic glade enclosed

Phoebe's view

mainly by forest trees.

John and I walk towards the wood this morning and find what we are looking for, clump after clump of four-inch stalks, fragile but erect, topped with white orbs. They will be the first snowdrops, planted probably a hundred years ago. In a few days the petals will open out and the rhythm of plant life will thrill us. Storms may rage, but if we work with nature, nature will not let us down.

Recipe for December: Apple Charlotte

We have loads of apples every autumn and use most of them. I often give them extra flavour with orange juice, a plum or two or a few blackberries. This traditional dish is very popular.

Ingredients

Serves four to six.

750 g/2 lb cooking apples, peeled and sliced

6 slices of white bread, buttered

240 g/8 oz Demerara sugar

juice of 2 oranges

Method

Cut the crusts off the bread and butter and place two slices at the bottom of a deepish baking dish, one that you can use at the table.

Add half the sliced apples, shower them with sugar and squeeze the juice of one orange over them.

Repeat all this once and press down the fruit. Leave enough sugar to sprinkle over this.

Top with the last two pieces of bread and butter, cut into strips, and sprinkle with sugar. Cover with buttered tinfoil.

Bake for 1½ hours at gas mark 5/190°C or 375°F, removing the tinfoil for long enough to brown the pudding.

Serve with pouring cream or brandy butter.

Index

The plants in the diary have well-known names used in garden centres.
For more information readers could consult a plant encyclopaedia.
References in **bold** indicate illustrations

Plan of Knockmore and its gardens in 1999 (Jeremy Williams)